Business and Retirement Guide to Belize

Business and Retirement Guide to Belize

Second Edition

BOB DHILLON
WITH FRED LANGAN

DUNDURN
TORONTO

Printer: Webcom

Library and Archives Canada Cataloguing in Publication

Dhillon, Bob, author
Business and retirement guide to Belize / Bob Dhillon with Fred Langan.
-- Second edition.

Includes index.
Issued in print and electronic formats.
ISBN 978-1-4597-4159-1 (softcover).--ISBN 978-1-4597-4160-7 (PDF).--
ISBN 978-1-4597-4161-4 (EPUB)

1. Belize--Guidebooks. 2. Retirement--Belize--Planning. 3. Investments, Foreign--Belize. I. Langan, F. F., author II. Title.

F1443.5.D45 2018 917.28204'5 C2017-906923-3
C2017-906924-1

1 2 3 4 5 22 21 20 19 18

Conseil des Arts du Canada
Canada Council for the Arts

We acknowledge the support of the **Canada Council for the Arts**, which last year invested $153 million to bring the arts to Canadians throughout the country, and the **Ontario Arts Council** for our publishing program. We also acknowledge the financial support of the **Government of Ontario**, through the **Ontario Book Publishing Tax Credit** and the **Ontario Media Development Corporation**, and the **Government of Canada**.

Nous remercions le **Conseil des arts du Canada** de son soutien. L'an dernier, le Conseil a investi 153 millions de dollars pour mettre de l'art dans la vie des Canadiennes et des Canadiens de tout le pays.

Care has been taken to trace the ownership of copyright material used in this book. The author and the publisher welcome any information enabling them to rectify any references or credits in subsequent editions.

—J. Kirk Howard, President

The publisher is not responsible for websites or their content unless they are owned by the publisher.

Printed and bound in Canada.

VISIT US AT

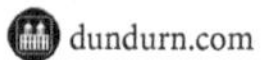 dundurn.com |  @dundurnpress | dundurnpress | 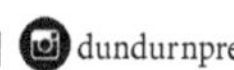 dundurnpress

Dundurn
3 Church Street, Suite 500
Toronto, Ontario, Canada
M5E 1M2

CONTENTS

	Introduction	7
Part I:	The Story of Belize	
1	Why Belize?	13
2	Paradise Past	21
3	Paradise Present	32
Part II:	Profiles	
4	The Pioneers	51
5	Other Entrepreneurs	71
6	What Makes Me Tick	79
Part III:	The Promise of Belize	
7	The Anatomy of Paradise	89
8	Freedom — Personal and Fiscal	96
9	Banking in Belize	106
10	Real Estate	119
11	Tourism	144
12	Easy Retirement in Belize	167
13	Other Opportunities for the Newcomer	179
14	The Last Word	201

	Acknowledgements	205
	Appendices	
Appendix A	Resources	209
Appendix B	Diplomatic and Government Contacts	214
Appendix C	Cruise Ship Activity	216
Appendix D	Belize Fact Sheet	218
	Photo Credits	221
	Index	222

INTRODUCTION

BELIZE. I told you so. When the first edition of this book came out in 2011 Belize was a hidden gem. There were only two U.S. airlines flying into the country. Now there are at least seven, along with two Canadian airlines, WestJet and Air Canada. Copa, Colombia's national airline, flies from Panama, and Avianca also flies into Belize. On a typical sunny day at Philip S.W. Goldson International Airport just outside of Belize City, there are six big jets lined up, disgorging or taking on passengers. The terminal has just been expanded to handle the rush to Belize. There could soon be two more international airports in Belize: one in Placencia in the south, the other at the north end of Ambergris Caye.

Why are all these people from the United States and Canada flocking to Belize? For the same reasons I came to the country many years ago. Once many of these visitors get a taste of Belize, they decide to move here to do business and/or retire.

The basics are still there. Belize is an English-speaking tropical paradise, with a Caribbean coast. Its water is as blue as a cloudless sky; it has an accessible rainforest, lost jungle cities, and a cost of living that makes it affordable for Americans, Canadians, and Europeans, as well as the emerging middle class of Mexico, Central America, and South America.

This book is an introduction to living and retiring in Belize, as well as a guide to doing business and owning property there. In this book I will try to make the reader familiar with the country, its beauty and friendly people, as well as its economic attractions. Belize is a movable feast — the better you get to know it, the more you will enjoy it.

I will also tell you everything you need to know about Belize, from why it is a great place to invest to why it is a safe and sensible place to retire. While I'm at it, I'll discuss everything from bonefish-fishing to Mayan ruins and throw in a bit of my own business philosophy.

• • • • •

Belize is a little-known tropical paradise. Many people I speak to think it's an island. It does have more than 400 islands, 108 of them uninhabited, but it is an independent nation on the mainland of Central America, bordered by Mexico — just south of Cancún — and Guatemala on the west and the Caribbean on the east. While it is the only English-speaking country in the region, it is a mix of many cultures, from Hispanic to ancient Mayan, and increasingly the home of modern expats.

This is the story in a nutshell. Belize is a few hours by plane from the largest cities in the United States and Canada. Property prices are a bargain; beachfront sites are still among the cheapest in the world. North Americans feel at home with Belize's laws. Its legal system is based on British common law. Belize is a

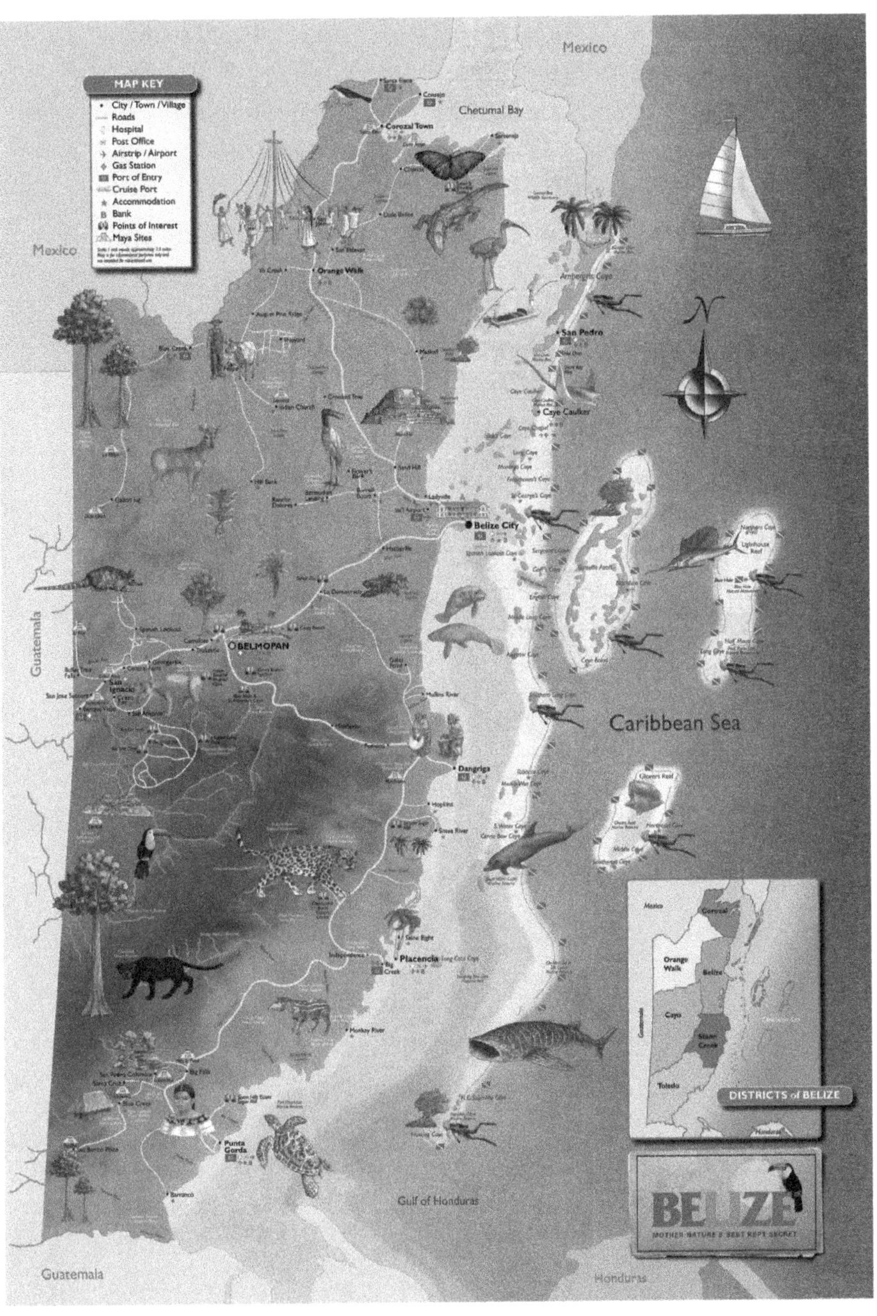

Map of Belize.

parliamentary democracy with no history of civil strife in a region exploding with it.

The economic situation in the country is also very positive. Foreign investors will feel comfortable with the way property is surveyed and transferred, along with many aspects of daily life with a pro-business government. The regulations for newcomers are simple; there are no taxes for retirees and other expats. The banking system allows you to operate a business at arm's length from your home jurisdiction.

The way I see it, Belize is still a ground-floor opportunity, as we say in the financial world. Why should you believe me? Well, I'm a successful real-estate entrepreneur and I'll give you details of my own ventures and how they mesh with the future of Belize. As I'll explain in detail throughout this book, the phrase the *Last Virgin Paradise* is not some marketing slogan; it's a reality.

PART I

THE STORY OF BELIZE

CHAPTER 1

WHY BELIZE?

BACK in the late 1990s, I went on a personal quest for a tropical paradise. For one thing, I wanted to get away from the cold winters of Canada's Alberta foothills, but I was too restless and too young to just head south and flop on a beach. First I tried the Caribbean, but it was overcrowded and overpriced. I was born too late to get started there. The best spots in the Caribbean were developed twenty or more years before I set out on my search.

The prime parts of Mexico were also overdeveloped. A forest of high-rises filled with tourists on package tours was not my idea of paradise. I prefer boutique hotels to mega-resorts. So I started looking in Central America. Costa Rica attracted me. What's not to like? It's peaceful and prosperous with everything from mountains to beaches and a democratic government to boot. I bought some land and embarked on a small venture.

Working in Western Canada, based in the free-market province of Alberta, I was spoiled, plain and simple. Titles pass easily through the system, as they do in the United States. Throughout much of the English-speaking world, the land survey regime is open, accurate, and, above all, easy to understand if you move from one place to another.

I considered Costa Rica. It is a wonderful country; however, I discovered, after spending time in the capital, San José, and travelling throughout the country, that it was already developed and prices were too high to get in on the ground floor. It seemed that the elevator had left the lobby long ago. Another problem is the country's legal and land-transfer systems. Frankly, it is a nightmare. For someone used to British common law and the transparency at work in countries such as Canada, the United States, and the United Kingdom, Costa Rica and other Central American countries, as well as Mexico, are very frustrating places to invest. The laws are based on the old Spanish civil code. Everything is in Spanish. It means lost time, money, and endless frustration.

You might think that because of all this I would have run. However, I was young and impatient to prove my investment savvy. So, I bought some property. It didn't take me long to realize that I had made a mistake. I took a hard look at the place and decided, after I owned property there for a short while, that the country was not for me. I quickly soured on Costa Rica as a place to live and make money.

While I waited to sell my property, I looked at the map, and saw Belize, formerly known as British Honduras. It wasn't a random flip through the atlas; a friend of mine tipped me off to the place.

• • • • •

My first trip to Belize convinced me it was the spot: an undeveloped, affordable paradise with everything going for it.

I quickly found that there were big differences between Spanish-speaking Costa Rica and English-speaking Belize, not the least of which was language. The common language and culture may explain the friendliness toward Americans and other English speakers in Belize — something that is noticeably different from the kind of grouchiness that exists in many parts of Spanish-speaking Latin America and even in some of the other English-speaking countries in the Caribbean.

From my experience — and I am a man of colour — they embrace all newcomers in Belize. In the town of San Pedro on the island of Ambergris Caye, where I spend a lot of my time when I'm in Belize, visitors are treated as if they are locals, which to my mind is the highest compliment. There are three main streets in the town, with the beach at one end, and the ferry terminal at the other. Simple. And that's how life is there, too. It is difficult to describe just how friendly the place really is without seeing it with your own eyes.

Not only is there respect for people of all types, there is also respect for private property here — something that is very much part of the British heritage of Belize. This means that the state doesn't act in

Belize banknote: The portrait of Queen Elizabeth II is on the currency of Belize, which says a lot about the country. The Belize dollar is tied to the U.S. dollar: one U.S. dollar buys two Belize dollars.

an arbitrary way, enacting laws that penalize foreign property owners, as often happens in neighbouring Mexico. This respect for property means the law makes it extremely difficult for people to seize property under so-called squatters' rights. That sets it apart from most Latin American countries.

Laid-Back and Affordable

One of the first things I noticed about Belize is how uncrowded it is: uninhabited islands dot the coastline; deserted beaches stretch for miles; and Mayan ruins, unseen by human eyes for centuries, lie hidden in the rainforests. New bits of its history are found in the jungle every year. It is estimated that only 5 to 10 percent of the Mayan ruins in Belize have been discovered.

Belize vs. Costa Rica and Barbados

	Belize	Costa Rica	Barbados
Population	387,879	4,930,258	292,336
Density	43/square mile	249/square mile	1,761/square mile
Area	8,867 square miles	19,729 square miles	167 square miles
Equal to area of	Massachusetts	West Virginia	More than double Washington, D.C.
Per capita GDP	\$8,200	\$16,400	\$17,100

Source: CIA World Factbook/Statistical Institute of Belize

The numbers tell the tale about the emptiness of Belize. Costa Rica, a country that doesn't exactly feel crowded, has a population of 4.9 million in a country of 19,729 square miles — about the same size as West Virginia. Belize has a population of 387,879 in a country of 8,867 square miles — about the same size as Massachusetts, home to 6.5 million people. Belize's population density is much lower than that of neighbouring countries in Central America and a tiny fraction of its crowded counterparts in the Caribbean.

Belize sits on the Caribbean Sea, its eastern coastline facing North America and the Caribbean islands. Some would say its soul is pointed in that direction, too. On the west and north it borders Mexico and Guatemala, both of which add a Spanish influence to places that are near the borders. Towns don't have names such as San Pedro and San Ignacio by accident. English might be the official language of the country, but Belize cannot and does not ignore its Central American neighbours; many people speak Spanish, or a mixture called Spanglish.

In Belize, it is Spanish at home, English at school.

"English is the official language, but 80 percent of the population speaks both languages, English and Spanish," says Manuel Heredia, the minister of tourism and civil aviation, who is himself of Hispanic background.

Some of the local English accents have a definite Spanish twang. Many others have the distinctive singsong rhythm of the Caribbean, even though Belize is eight hundred miles from Jamaica and even farther away from most of the English-speaking Caribbean.

• • • • •

Cancún is four hundred miles from Belize City and just a four- to five-hour drive from northern Belize, most of it on the Mexican highway system. But Cancún is a world away from Belize when it comes to tourism and development. Even if it wanted to be — and the people and government of Belize abhor the thought — this country could never be another Cancún, with its crowded towers jammed into thin strips of land bordering the sea.

Belize isn't dense with high-rise hotels, and it never will be; in most places there is a four-storey height restriction. One of the things I always tell people about this country is that the tallest buildings in all of Belize are still two Mayan temples.

Belize is custom-made for smaller projects, which is why development is being well thought out and meticulously planned. The ideal projects are boutique resorts aimed at those who frequent such places as Saint-Tropez on the French Riviera or St. Barts in the Caribbean.

The smallest hotel in San Pedro, my base in Belize, has one room. A twenty-minute boat ride up the coast is Azul, a resort with a spectacular restaurant and a clear view of the country's impressive reef, the second largest in the world. We discuss the reef in detail in Chapter 3. Owners Jeff Spiegel and his wife came here from San Francisco in 2005, where he ran a punk-rock record label and she was in the design business. Azul has just two luxury suites, each with its own stretch of beach. There is a helicopter pad on the six-acre property, which gives you an idea of their clientele.

Belize is a land made for developers, big and small. One example is Gabriel Kirchberger, a businessman from Brantford, Ontario, who owns luxury rental properties on Costa del Sol and who is redeveloping Brahma Blue, a four-storey luxury building. He loves my island, Costa de Sol, because it so close to San Pedro, but at the same time just far enough away.

"Over here on this side, it is total darkness; on the other side you can see the lights of the town at night, even hear the music. You see life, but you're detached from it," says Gabriel.

Gabriel only started coming to Belize in 2013. He says there is a real buzz about the country back in Canada. "I did a lot of research on Belize and I think the more you talk about Belize, the more people know Belize, and everybody in Canada talks about the country. Of course not a lot of people have been here but a lot of people will come. WestJet flies in twice a week now and it is an up-and-coming destination."

Despite the growing number of tourists, there are no giant hotels being built. Brahma Blue is just a four-storey building; nothing is going much higher. The mayor of Ambergris Caye, Danny Guerrero, says building heights are part of the new master plan for the island. "We definitely don't want to go over five storeys," says Danny.

Another interesting development is being done by Ricardo and Giovanni Pelayo. Ricardo is CEO of Atlantic International Bank. The company is funding Amber Sunset Jungle Resort, which is located at Mile 59 on the George Price Highway in the village of Unitedville, in the Cayo District, in the western part of Belize. Karim Hakimi, the founder of the Hakim Optical chain in Canada, has also begun to invest in Belize. He has developed a property called Turneffe Island Resort.

As already mentioned, Belize is sparsely populated, with its population just 387,879. The place never feels crowded, even when visitors congregate in places such as San Pedro. It has fewer tourists than any country in Central America.

Although tourism is growing, people want to maintain that sense of space and for that reason people don't want growth to go unchecked. I see Belize as being where Costa Rica was thirty years ago, though with a much smaller population. Even with development, Belize will retain its character: it is uncrowded; increasingly becoming the oasis of choice for people who have seen one paradise after another ruined by overdevelopment.

Belize isn't just a paradise to escape to and soak up the sun, however. There are opportunities for a wide range of investors: people who want a safe upmarket vacation home; consultants who are looking for a low-cost base for global assignments or other businesses; and developers who are interested in planned, low-density communities.

• • • • •

Not only is the country beautiful and land plentiful, the weather is perfect, too. Weather experts say the currents in the waters off the coast combined with the shape of the Yucatán Peninsula to the north direct most hurricanes away from the country. Though Belize is hit by a few major storms every few years, more and more of the buildings are now constructed to properly withstand these. In fact, while on the subject, housing in my development on Costa del Sol off San Pedro is built on a concrete core to the latest standards, all designed to withstand hurricanes. Most other developers of condos and hotels in the area are doing the same.

CHAPTER 2

PARADISE PAST

WHAT'S a country like Belize doing in a place like this?

It is an English-speaking island floating in a Spanish sea. Tucked into the Yucatán Peninsula under Mexico, with its western border running along Guatemala, you have to wonder how this small country stayed out of the Spanish empire that became Latin America.

When you go back to the conquistadors, the Spaniards who took over the Americas in the sixteenth century, you learn they missed this little stretch of land along the Caribbean coast. That's not exactly true, though. If you read the Mayan history of Belize, you'll discover that the resistance of the Mayan inhabitants to the Spanish soldiers, led by Hernán Cortés, was one reason this sliver of Central America was left untouched by the conquistadors.

Some rough-and-ready Brits settled on the coast of Belize, however. One of the first was Peter Wallace, a Scottish privateer authorized by King James I to harass the Spanish Main, as the Caribbean was then called. In 1603, Wallace built a small settlement where Belize City now stands. Shipwrecked British sailors set up residence in 1638 and adventurers in search of treasure followed.

But the only treasure they found along the coast was a tree known as logwood. It grew in abundance and was shipped back to Britain and Europe to be used as the source of a dye for the wool trade.

The string of islands and coral reefs that now delight visitors and residents of Belize were then an ideal hiding spot for the pirates and privateers who were after the gold in the ships bringing treasure home from the Spanish empire in the Americas. The coves and offshore islands of Belize, now tropical retreats, remained a pirate haven for more than a hundred years. In his book *Belize: A Concise History*, P.A.B. Thomson writes, "William Teach, better known as Blackbeard, is said to have refitted his ship on Turneffe Island, off the barrier reef, in 1717." Known today as Turneffe Atoll,

Historical Timeline of Belize

Mayan civilization thrived for 1,500 years.

300–900	Peak period of Mayan culture.
1519	Arrival of Spanish and subsequent destruction of remaining Mayan culture.
1638	Lumber exploitation begins.
1650	British privateers settle islands and coast of Belize.
1798	British Navy sees off the Spanish in the Battle of St. George's Caye.
1807	Slave trade abolished.
1862	Becomes colony of British Honduras.
1973	Name changed to Belize. The standard explanation: it is Mayan, from the word *belix* (muddy water), and is named after the muddy water of the Belize River.
1981	Belize becomes independent country.

Source: Government of Belize and *Belize: A Concise History*, P.A.B. Thomson.

it is a fishing paradise renowned for bonefish, wahoo, and barracuda, which historians say were probably the main staple of the pirates' diet.

As well as sending privateers, Britain also sent settlers. It signed many treaties with Spain, giving the English settlers the right to live in the Spanish colony. These treaties even allowed the settlers to live under local rule. Among these rules was a law that restricted the settlers' agriculture to subsistence farming, though they could still log.

Back in Britain some clever entrepreneur found an easier way to dye wool than dragging trees five thousand miles across the ocean. Demand for logwood fell, but the enterprising loggers found a new way to make money: mahogany. The forests of Belize were filled with dense hardwood. Fine furniture was fashionable back in England, and, as any fan of *Antiques Roadshow* will tell you, mahogany was the wood of choice.

The original settlers learned to get along and held meetings to settle local disputes. This situation persisted for some time, but at a certain point the Bay of Honduras came under the rule of the governor of Jamaica. In 1765 Rear Admiral Burnaby, the naval commander there, laid down the rules known as Burnaby's Code, which gave limited powers to elected magistrates in the outpost along the coast of Central America, in effect making it one of the earliest democracies in the British Empire, though it was not even officially a colony until the next century.

Spain always laid claim to the area, but the power of the Royal Navy kept the Bay of Honduras British. This power struggle culminated in the 1798 Battle of St. George's Caye, just off the coast of what is now Belize

City. The two-hour battle was won by the sixteen-gun sloop *Merlin* and two other Royal Navy ships sent from Jamaica. It was the last Spanish attack on the Bay of Honduras. Today, the event is celebrated as St. George's Caye Day on September 10.

After the British had secured it, however, the country slipped back into being a forgotten outpost. Throughout the eighteenth century, it had been only a minor part of the British Empire, which was being expanded elsewhere.

The population did grow during the American Revolution, though, when some Brits were expelled by the Spanish from Nicaragua's Mosquito Coast — named for the Miskito people, not the ubiquitous insect. Then a couple of West India regiments posted to Belize decided to remain once their tour of duty was done.

In the 1860s, the territory's name was changed to British Honduras, and in 1871 it officially became a

Belize Harbour in the nineteenth century.

British colony. This also marked the time when neighbouring Guatemala stated its land claims in Belize and the surrounding territory so it could expand to the Caribbean. These efforts proved fruitless, however.

Belize was a part of the British Empire, but was ignored. While the other British possessions in the Caribbean and the rest of the world gained their independence, sleepy British Honduras kept its colonial status.

Development was slow. It took until 1963 for the population to reach a hundred thousand. Tourism as we know it now was non-existent; only the keen scuba divers and sports fishermen would venture to this little-known corner of Central America.

In 1973, British Honduras officially changed its name to Belize, and eight years later gained its independence, becoming a member of the Commonwealth. Guatemala recognized Belize as a sovereign nation in 1992.

Belize remains allied with Britain, which provides the country military guarantees, as well as a small military force. In return, the country provides a jungle training base for the British Army. During the worrying border squabbles with Guatemala, Britain based as many as six thousand troops in Belize, including a squadron of Harrier jump jets that could operate from clearings in the jungle.

While relying on Britain for protection from external threats, Belize has a small military of its own, the two-thousand-member Belize Defence Force, which is used

> "If the world has any ends, British Honduras would certainly be one of them. It is not on the way from anywhere to anywhere else. It has no strategic value. It is all but uninhabited."
>
> — Aldous Huxley, 1934

for border protection, as well as watching for illegal drug and firearms trafficking.

In the history of the Bay of Honduras, British Honduras, and Belize, what stands out is how the rule of law, democracy, and tolerance evolved. The first public meetings became a legislature. The magistrates empowered under Burnaby's Code became courts, including a Supreme Court established as early as 1819. Unlike any other country on mainland America, Belize achieved its independence without the shedding of blood.

Belize's Hidden Mayan Treasures

This later tradition of peaceful evolution is, however, a far cry from the early history of Belize when the country was the centre of warring city-states in the Mayan empire. There are still Maya in modern Belize, but they are just a part of what has become a uniquely diverse population, different from anything else in Central America or the Caribbean.

Belize holds as many Mayan treasures as Mexico or Guatemala, and the jungle yields more every year. The most recent discovery was an underground city. Just twelve miles outside San Ignacio, howler monkeys sit in trees that are part of the jungle that took over the Mayan city of El Pilar. Temples in the city are connected by man-made underground tunnels twenty feet or more below the jungle.

Archaeological secrets add a new dimension to this Central American paradise. There are enough natural wonders to keep a curious person busy for a lifetime — one of the many reasons the place fascinates me. One of Belize's top archaeologists says that there are more ancient

Caana. This Mayan temple is the tallest building in Belize.

buildings in the country than modern ones. The tallest ancient structure in Belize is the Mayan temple at Caracol. Hidden in the rainforest for centuries and discovered only in 1937, Caracol is a town that once held 150,000 people, almost half the current population of Belize. Twenty-four miles outside of Caracol is the temple of El Castillo, which is the second tallest building in the country.

When the Maya dominated what is now called Central America, their cities were as complex as any in Europe during the Dark Ages, and far more populous. Most people know of the legacy the Maya left in Mexico and other Central American countries. But because Belize is an English-speaking country, there is a misconception that it doesn't share the history of its Spanish-speaking neighbours. It certainly doesn't have the more recent violent political history of neighbouring Mexico, Guatemala, Honduras, or El Salvador. There has never been a political revolution or civil war in modern Belize. What it does share with those four countries, however, is Mayan culture. The Maya were part of what is called the pre-Columbian age, that is, before Christopher Columbus arrived in the Caribbean in 1492. Their civilization reached its peak hundreds of years before the Spanish appeared.

Unlike the Aztec in northern Mexico or the Inca of Peru, Mayan civilization did not have one ruler, but was fifty city-states, each with its own king. Many of the cities had fortifications or even moats. The Maya were warriors who engaged in power struggles between city-states that lasted generations. Like the Egyptian pyramids, the massive temples were built using the labour of thousands, from the artisans who carved the friezes into rock to the slaves who pulled the giant stones into place.

Mayan civilization flourished from 250 to 900 CE, developing a written language, among other innovations. Among other things, the Maya understood the mathematical concept of zero, something the Romans did not work out until much later. The Maya didn't use metal tools; however, they were still able to construct massive stone buildings and other complex structures. They adapted the wheel, but did not use it for transport; rather, they employed it for simple things such as children's toys. Their advanced calendar foretold the end of the world in 2012. We missed that target.

After flourishing for centuries, the Mayan civilization suddenly seemed to vanish, perhaps crumbling under the weight of overpopulation. "The Mayans [sic] were victims of their own success," noted one archaeologist.

Examples of Mayan Sites

Actun Tunichil Muknal: This spectacular cave and its ruins requires a strenuous hike in the jungle. Not for the faint of heart.

Altun Ha: Spectacular temples an hour from Belize City. There are three square miles of Mayan ruins.

Altun Ha Temple.

Cahal Pech: This site is thought to have been an outpost of the local aristocracy, guarding river routes into the area. Fascinating Mayan caves. Resort accommodation is available in nearby San Ignacio.

Caracol: Massive pyramids dominate a lost city that once covered two hundred square miles; today it is about thirty square miles. It was discovered by a logger in 1937.

El Pilar: This site near San Ignacio is still being uncovered. Occupied from 700 BCE to 1000 CE, El Pilar reveals something of Mayan daily life.

Lamanai: In northern Belize and accessible by boat, this city-state lasted into the Spanish era.

"But they left behind the marks of an amazing civilization. Not just the buildings. The Mayan calendar was the most accurate in the ancient world, more accurate than those used by the Romans, the Indians, or the Chinese."

While theories abound, many historians and archaeologists believe that the Maya hit their peak around 750 to 800 CE, with a population of approximately two million in what is modern-day Belize. Overpopulation was perhaps their downfall. Historians say the Maya couldn't feed millions of people. Crops failed, either due to overuse of the land or by a natural drought. In the caves and temples, there are signs of ritual human sacrifices, perhaps trying to appease the gods in the hope of a richer harvest.

It didn't work.

Evidence suggests that there were as many as eight to ten million Mayan people living throughout Central America at the peak of that civilization's glory; there are perhaps two million Maya today. Although the civilization collapsed, the Mayas' descendants still live in Belize and the surrounding countries of Central America, preserving their culture and their love of nature.

"Studying the Maya is important, and there is a wealth of archaeological material in Belize," said the late Tom Grimshaw, a Belize citizen who emigrated from the United States, and made his living running a firm that did detailed environmental work for developers. He pointed out that knowing more about the Maya is not just curiosity; it can tell us a lot about ourselves. "Knowing more about the world of the Maya helps us know how they lived on the natural resource base here."

Grimshaw pointed out that Mayan sites are protected by law. I believe even more protection is needed to make sure their history is safe from development and looting.

There are still places in Belize where half the population is descended from the Maya. Their temples are spectacular, and are located in more remote places than those in nearby countries that were also part of the Mayan empire. Because Belize remained relatively isolated, most of the Mayan ruins have been left alone, hidden by the jungle. On one of my many outings to see a particular Mayan temple, I was the only person there.

While some of the major Mayan sites are easier to get to than others, you still must go with a guide. For example, you can drive to Actun Tunichil Muknal (ATM), but some of the more isolated ruins can be accessed only by trekking through the jungle. If you want to do it the easy way, fly in by helicopter. Whatever sites are accessible to you, I would highly recommend visiting as many as you can.

CHAPTER 3

PARADISE PRESENT

MY personal history, as a Sikh born in Japan, who moved to Liberia in West Africa, and then to Western Canada, has taught me the importance of culture and ethnic diversity, one of the abiding strengths of Belize. The people of Belize have been formed by their history and their geography.

The literacy rate is 82.3 percent, right up there with the standard of the developed world. The centuries-old tradition of self-government and respect for the rule of law makes it welcoming for newcomers from countries with the same common-law and democratic traditions. There is none of the instability that characterizes some neighbouring Latin American and Caribbean countries.

According to author and former British high commissioner Peter Thomson, Belize is "an unusually heterogeneous society." He was so impressed by the country that after his stay he wrote *Belize: A Concise History*, which documents how Belize's history has brought together disparate groups of people tolerant of one another so that none have dominated.

Of these groups, the Garifuna is the one that is most likely to be unfamiliar to most people. In fact, the term

Origin of the Garifuna

"The Black Caribs (then spelt Charibs, now called Garifuna) ... originated from a mingling in the eastern Caribbean between aboriginal Red Caribs and escaped African slaves. They had been transported to the island of Ruatan in the Gulf of Honduras in 1797 following rebellions in Dominica and St. Vincent. By 1802, 150 of them had migrated to the coast [of present-day Belize].... Physically more African than Carib, they remained culturally distinct from the much larger number of Africans brought to the territory as slaves."

– P.A.B. Thomson, *Belize: A Concise History*

Belize Population Mix

Mestizos	Descendants for whom their Spanish heritage is dominant	52.9%
Creoles	Descendants of white settlers and Caribbean blacks	25.9%
Maya	Descendants of the Mayan people	11.3%
Garifunas	Descendants of escaped slaves and native Caribbean tribes	3.9%
Mennonites	Canadian settlers descended from the European religious order	3.6%
Asians		1.0%
Other		2.7%

Source: CIA World Factbook

Garifuna is so unusual that it is not even listed in the giant edition of the *Oxford English Dictionary*, though it does appear on Wikipedia.

Today, most of the Garifuna live in the southern part of Belize. Although they make up only a small part of the country's population, Garifuna Settlement Day is a national holiday in Belize, celebrated every year on November 19.

• • • • •

The new immigrants to Belize are North Americans and Europeans. The Concord Group, a California-based real-estate research firm, in an analysis of the Belize real-estate market, divided the newcomers into three categories: Snowbirds, Weekend Getaways, and Jet-setters.

Snowbirds — either on extended holidays or retired — are vacationers aged forty to seventy-five who come from the colder regions of North America and Europe. They are business owners, telecommuters, and retirees looking for a second home in a warmer climate to escape winter. They want to live in a stable country, with few business and language barriers, that is a reasonable travel distance by air from home. Belize certainly meets those criteria. And the retirement rules in Belize make the country even more attractive.

Weekend Getaways are professionals, executives, and the self-employed, mostly from American and Canadian cities. They are wealthy, young, and in a hurry. Not only do they want facilities such as marinas, but these active business people are also attracted by the ease of doing business, as well as the proximity to major urban areas by direct flights.

Jet-setters prefer the unusual. In Belize they can dive in the morning and take a helicopter to a Mayan site in the afternoon. Not for everyone, but it's there if you have the cash and the curiosity. They are the smallest and the richest group. Jet-setters are not just from North America, they now also come from Europe, Asia, and the Middle East. These people are top business leaders, celebrities, socialites, and even government leaders. They want different things from their leisure time and travel a lot, often in pursuit of the next hot spot. They love the weather and look forward to the exotic aspects of Belize, including new luxurious five-star hotels. A few of the super-rich buy islands in Belize, the ultimate in beachfront privacy. A combination of the two is Cayo Espanto, a five-star resort on a private island off the coast of San Pedro.

There is another group the report didn't mention: the European backpackers. One of their favourite parts of Belize is the laid-back Caye Caulker. These are mainly young people from crowded, civilized Old Europe who are hypnotized by the beauty and unspoiled wilderness of Belize. When someone from Stuttgart or London finds they can wander into the jungle hours after getting off the plane and see birds unknown in Europe and maybe even a jaguar in the wild, they are hooked for life.

On a warm February day, I was sitting in a bakery in San Pedro when I struck up a conversation with four Italians on their first trip to Belize. What they liked was pretty straightforward. "The ocean and the beach," said Illaria. She added that she liked how relaxed things were. "And the friendly people."

All of these different types are discovering Belize, and a lot of the things that they are looking for are only just starting to appear, from yacht rentals to high-speed internet.

Advanced (and affordable) medical services, for example, are another thing that visitors to the country are increasingly looking for. Belize has a state medical system, but there is a growing number of private clinics that cater to visitors, as well as doctors who perform surgery at rates much cheaper than in the United States. It's not perfect — there is a lot of room for improvement. But, as I keep repeating, there is still a lot of opportunity here to get in on what is effectively the ground floor.

• • • • •

Whatever the reason for their trip, travellers to Belize find an amazing country.

The weather, of course, is one of the big reasons Belize is so attractive. Even in late December and January it can be downright cold in places such as southern Florida (they have frost warnings for oranges, don't they?), but in Belize it is always warm. Here's a chart that details when it rains, when it shines, and what the temperature is likely to be.

Weather in Belize

Month	Avg. Daily High (°F/°C)	Avg. Daily Low (°F/°C)	Rain (inches/mm)	% Days with Rain
January	79.6/26.4	69.9/21.0	4.54/115	40
February	80.5/27.0	71.1/21.7	2.45/62	32
March	83.0/28.3	73.8/23.2	2.04/52	22
April	85.0/29.4	76.0/24.4	3.19/81	20
May	87.2/30.6	78.6/25.9	4.15/105	21
June	86.6/30.3	78.8/26.0	8.82/224	52
July	86.3/30.2	78.6/25.9	8.48/215	41
August	86.4/30.2	78.3/25.7	6.81/173	43
September	85.9/29.9	77.4/25.4	9.61/244	48
October	84.3/29.0	75.3/24.0	9.66/245	45
November	82.4/28.0	73.1/22.8	7.3/185	41
December	80.3/26.8	70.7/21.5	6.57/167	45

NOTE: Weather is average for Belize. Coastal areas are drier.

Belize Weather Facts

Since 1889, when Belize weather records were first formally maintained, there have been:

- Twenty hurricanes (about one hurricane every six years)
- Thirty-one tropical storms (about one tropical storm every 3.75 years)

Of the twenty hurricanes:

- Nine were in September
- Eight were in October
- Two were in July
- One was in November

Belize is like no other place I've ever been. No exaggeration. I can't think of another spot I have visited — and I've lived and travelled all over the world — that has so much beauty and diversity packed into such a compact package.

You can see the spectacular scenery from the air. The small planes of Maya Island Air and Tropic Air fly low as they take you to the landing fields in the jungle or to the cayes off the coast. From the slow-moving aircraft you see some of the 108 uninhabited islands, just patches of green in the sea, places without even a goat. And it is one of those empty pieces of paradise, just off San Pedro, where I am developing Costa del Sol and its sister property, the Platinum Coast (see chapter 10: Real Estate). To be precise, Costa del Sol is the part of the development facing San Pedro. The Platinum Coast, the prime property, looks out over the Bay of Chetumal. Belize also means long stretches of deserted beaches, mountains, jungles, reefs, and atolls.

Some of the Many Rivers in Belize

- **Belize River:** From the blue Caribbean to the green jungle in a few hours
- **Macal River:** Drift past Mayan ruins and the Belize Botanical Gardens
- **Monkey River:** Crocodiles and birds, and, yes, even monkeys
- **Sibun River:** Canoe up a wildlife sanctuary just thirty miles from Belize City
- **Sittee River:** A birdwatching paradise

As well as those, there is something else that most of the guidebooks neglect to mention: the rivers, many of them as isolated and remote as the rainforest. The first time I went up one of these little-travelled rivers I found it a calming and breathtaking experience that helped shut off the rest of world.

All that water is boon for agriculture. Citrus and banana plantations — detailed later — need tremendous amounts of water and in Belize they do not have a problem with that.

Belize has an area of 8,867 square miles, making it just a bit bigger than nearby El Salvador (8,123 square miles), which hugs the Pacific Ocean on the other side of Guatemala. By the way, El Salvador has a population of more than 6.1 million, sixteen times that of Belize. Even today it is the emptiness of Belize that strikes the visitor. The population of Belize City, the old capital, is 62,582, while that of the current capital, Belmopan, is just 21,814. The government lists those as the only two cities in the country. The other population centres are seven towns, such as San Ignacio or San Pedro, for example, or villages like Caye Caulker.

Water, Water, Everywhere

Belize is awash in fresh water. A country that faces the salty Caribbean Sea, it is blessed with abundant fresh water; water flows from the Maya Mountains to the Caribbean providing fresh water for banana and citrus plantations and residential use.

Then there is rain. The rainy season in Belize replenishes aquifers after long dry periods that run from January to May. Annual rainfall ranges from 60 inches in the north of the country, to 160 inches in the south of the country, peaking in Punta Gorda, according to the National Meteorological Service of Belize.

Belize's prosperous agricultural sector relies on the rich supply of fresh water. Indeed, on a banana plantation I visited recently, there are drainage schemes to draw off water if there is too much of it.

In a world where access to fresh water is a worry, Belize has a rich, constantly renewed supply. Water, water, everywhere.

Huge swathes of Belize — almost 40 percent of the country's total area — are set aside as national parks. Its rainforests are protected from the type of slash-and-burn developments that have ruined other tropical paradises. Costa Rica likes to boast of its national parks, and they are impressive. But as a percentage of total area, Belize has set aside a much greater portion of its territory than any other country in Central America.

The Great Blue Hole is one of those amazing natural phenomena that make the cover of tourists' guides. It is a stunning jewel set in a ring of corals. Measuring one thousand feet across and 412 feet deep, this ocean-floor sinkhole is believed to be the world's largest blue hole. Divers descend into the tranquil abyss to see geological wonders and fascinating marine life. Giant stalactites, dripstone sheets, and columns adorn the gallery at the southern rim of the Great Blue Hole.

The Natural Wonders of Belize

Belize Barrier Reef

The largest reef in the western hemisphere and second largest in the world, this 185-mile coastal wonder has been designated a World Heritage Site by UNESCO. It encompasses over four hundred islands, white sand beaches, fringing and patch reefs, and over a hundred species of coral.

Great Blue Hole

The "Blue Hole" is located in the centre of Lighthouse Reef Atoll, which is about fifty miles due east of Belize City. Originally a cave, the roof fell in some ten thousand years ago, as the land receded into the sea. Almost a perfectly circular hole, 1,000 feet in diameter, it is 412 feet deep.

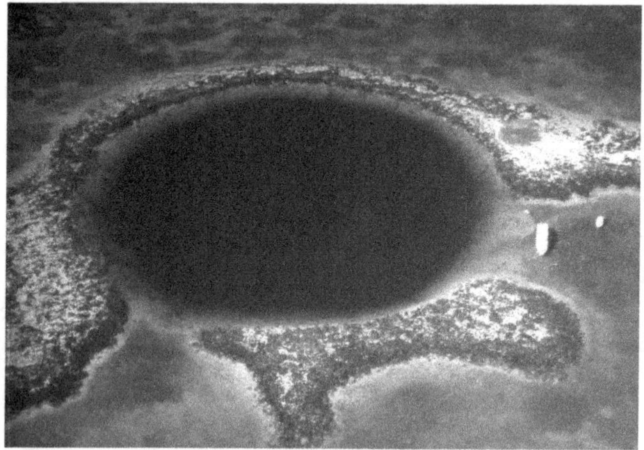

The Great Blue Hole: One of the natural wonders of Belize.

St. Herman's Blue Hole National Park

St. Herman's Blue Hole National Park is twelve miles southeast of Belmopan on the Hummingbird Highway. This inland blue hole is a popular recreational spot, where water on its way underground from a tributary to the Sibun River emerges in a karst sinkhole. The pool, from which the park receives its name, is an evocative sapphire blue, and about twenty-five feet deep. Resuming its underground run beneath a natural jungle setting, the stream disappears into a large cave, St. Herman's Cave.

Like the pool, St. Herman's Cave is within the boundaries of the reserve. This cave has archaeological importance because the Maya occupied it during the Classic Period. Pottery vessels, spears, and torches are among some of the artifacts that have been recovered by the Department of Archaeology. Visitors to St. Herman's do not need the usual government permission to explore caves.

Since St. Herman's Blue Hole National Park contains some 575 acres of primary and secondary forest, there is a significant opportunity to observe birds and animals, as well as a plethora of flora.

Hol Chan Marine Reserve

The Hol Chan Marine Reserve focuses on the Hol Chan (Mayan for *Little Channel*) Cut, which is in the barrier reef, some four miles southeast of San Pedro Town, Ambergris Caye. Established in 1987, the reserve, the first of its kind in Central America, includes three square miles in four distinctive zones.

Cockscomb Basin Wildlife Sanctuary

Situated within the shadows of the Maya Mountains, the sanctuary encompasses a hundred thousand acres of tropical moist forest that rises from 300 feet above sea level to approximately 3,675 feet at the summit of Victoria Peak.

Established in 1984 as a reserve to protect a large population of jaguars, as well as other resident wildlife, the sanctuary is also known as The Jaguar Preserve. The sanctuary being home to numerous members of the cat family, there is also a large population of mammals and birds to support the food chain. Therefore, even though you may not see jaguars or other carnivores during your visit, the opportunity to see herbivorous animals, a multitude of birds, and beautiful flora is always present.

Birdwatchers' paradise. A pair of scarlet macaws fly over the rainforest.

Mountain Pine Ridge

The Mountain Pine Ridge is three hundred square miles of forest reserve, south of the Western Highway in the Cayo District. The Mountain Pine Ridge is home to the Hidden Valley Falls (also known as Thousand-Foot Falls), the Rio On river, the Rio On Pools, and the Rio Frio Cave and Nature Trail, as well as numerous small streams and waterfalls. It is also the location of one of the country's largest Mayan sites, Caracol. Caracol's largest pyramid, Caana (Sky Place), rises 140 feet and is the tallest man-made structure in all of Belize.

Spectacular waterfalls and abundant electricity: no water shortage in Belize.

In 1971, millions of viewers were introduced to the mysterious Great Blue Hole through the television series *The Undersea World of Jacques Cousteau*. Today, it's one of the world's best destinations for scuba diving. Blue Hole Natural Monument is one the seven wonders of Belize's World Heritage Site. The Belize Barrier Reef Reserve System, which covers a total of 237,962 acres, displays classic examples of reef types: fringing, barrier, and atoll.

The United Nations World Heritage Committee formally adopted seven marine protected areas along the Belize Barrier Reef and its adjacent atolls as a World Heritage Site under UNESCO. Blue Hole Natural Monument is part of it.

The terrain in Belize is as varied as that of any country in Central America. Along the northwestern coast there are warm beaches, and cayes (pronounced *keys*) and atolls as beautiful as any in the Caribbean, minus the commercialism and crowds.

The comparison with Caribbean countries is even starker: crowded Barbados has 1,704 people per square mile, not including tourists; even a relatively large island such as Jamaica has a population density of 656 people per square mile.

Belize is also much cheaper than other countries in the Caribbean, whether you want to rent or buy. Renting a two-bedroom condo can run from $1,000 to $2,000 a month. Buying a quality condo in this area runs $350,000 and up, and the average condo fee runs from $250 to $400 a month. It's cheaper in other parts of Belize. Properties are more liquid in San Pedro and the rest of Ambergris Caye because of the popularity of the place.

Getting to the Natural Wonders of Belize

"Blue Hole Natural Monument and the Lighthouse Reef Atoll are 55 miles east of Belize City. Several PADI (Professional Association of Diving Instructors) dive operators visit Half Moon Caye Natural Monument out of San Pedro, Caye Caulker, Hopkins, or Belize City. There are also charter services and live-aboard dive ships, as well as island lodges that provide packages that get you there." Local live-aboard dive ships are now required to anchor in designated areas as their anchors have caused irreversible damage to the reef. Air charters are available if you want a good aerial view of the Blue Hole and Lighthouse Reef Atoll.

Source: The Belize Audubon Society

Electricity is expensive, but you can let the wind do the work. One retiree gets a breeze in his condo on the water and that means he doesn't use his air conditioning much, so his monthly bill is BZ$125 (US$62.50). "My condo faces northeast and the trade winds just blow through, so I don't need the air conditioning."

He keeps a close tab on expenses and knows what is cheaper and what is more expensive than back home. Property taxes are ridiculously low. On a $500,000 condo property, taxes are about $150 a year.

San Pedro

My little piece of paradise is just off Ambergris Caye, Belize's largest island, twenty miles off the mainland. You can get to San Pedro on Ambergris Caye from the main international airport at Belize City in a comfortable single engine plane — a twelve-minute flight — or take a short ferry ride. There is also a high-speed ferry operating from Chetumal, Mexico, to San Pedro. Called the Water Jets International (http://belizewatertaxiexpress.com), it is $50 one way or $95 return.

San Pedro, which is really a large village on the island of Ambergris Caye, is just a short hop from Belize City. Since the local planes cruise at around 1,500 feet, you get a spectacular view of the unspoiled islands and the shallow aquamarine sea inside the barrier reef. One of the first things most people notice as they come in to land are the neat, bright-coloured houses. Ambergris Caye is twenty-five miles long and four-and-a-half miles wide. It was once attached to the Yucatán Peninsula, but the Maya dug a canal that separates it to this day. One sign of progress is San Pedro's modern air terminal, which replaced a quaint wooden building. The paved landing strip also handles private planes. The workhorse of both Tropic Air Belize and Maya Island Air is the Cessna Caravan.

Belize's cayes and towns are connected by air.

In 2000, San Pedro Town's population was just 4,267; today it's 18,440 and yet it's not crowded. There are only ten streets in San Pedro, so it's tough to get lost. And despite its being incredibly laid-back, there are grocery stores, banks with cash machines, and dozens of restaurants and busy bars.

In many ways, San Pedro is a peaceful backwater, a land of golf carts, dusty back streets, laughing schoolchildren in their British-style uniforms, warm water, and restaurants rich with local fish. And just a two-minute boat ride across the channel is Costa del Sol, part of my three-thousand-acre property, which consists of one large island and several smaller ones.

Don't let the town's outward sleepiness fool you; it is also the focal point of tourist development in Belize. The minister of tourism, Manuel Heredia, a fisherman who is liable to show up barefoot to a business meeting in San Pedro, told me that half the tourists to Belize head to San Pedro, and the island pays 70 percent of all of the nation's hotel taxes. Heredia is the member of parliament for San Pedro and Ambergris Caye and he is working on ways to make Belize more attractive to investors, particularly North American retirees.

San Pedro is safe. You can wander around the streets at night or walk along the beach without a worry. There's something about an island that makes people think twice about crime. The property we're restoring is pretty wild, even though it's close to San Pedro. There are many creatures you only read about in tourist guides, including the reclusive ocelot — it's just a bit bigger than a house cat, with jaguar-like markings. There are herds of small deer around. I'm not saying it's a zoo; these animals are wild and pretty elusive, but they are there.

On the Caribbean side of Ambergris Caye is the barrier reef. Oddly enough, one of the best times to see it is at night. We often go out in a locally made twenty-five-foot flat-bottomed boat custom-built for the shallow water. Nothing is as spectacular as a fifteen- to thirty-minute trip. First there's the channel through the untouched mangrove swamps, then under a bridge and out into the open water, kept calm by the barrier reef. The waves hitting the reef are incandescent in the moonlight, providing a kind of natural light show all the way up the coast.

When the sun goes down, San Pedro stays up. In the early evening, as the rising moon shimmers across the Caribbean, families, locals, and visitors eat in the beachfront restaurants. Later in the evening the bars and restaurants come alive; San Pedro is safe and fun, a kind of Ibiza on the Caribbean coast.

PART II

PROFILES

CHAPTER 4

THE PIONEERS

A lot of people ask me what it's like to live in Belize. Well, by this point you can guess my answer. The reality is that it depends on your lifestyle. If you can't live without the buzz of places such as New York or Shanghai or you feel the need of the cultural comfort zone of Florida or Arizona, then Belize is not the place for you.

It's another thing if you want to live somewhere that's warm and peaceful. Belize isn't only for people who are ready to retire. I'm decades away from retiring, so I only spend part of my time here. But when I am here, I'm busy. That's the way I like to lead my life, and it's relaxing to do business here rather than back in Canada.

Belize might be a sleepy paradise, but it is an active place filled with fascinating people. I've found there is a seemingly endless supply of characters to make life interesting. For one thing, you're not limited by language, since Belize is an English-speaking country. Then there are the expats — people who have decided to make Belize their home.

• • • • •

In 1979 a group of young men, some from Texas, a few from Canada, decided to build a hotel in Belize, and they chose a spot at the southern tip of Ambergris Caye. Even though it was a modest venture at first, just ten casitas, or small guest cabins, and a dining room, it was ambitious for the era.

They opened for business in 1981, the same year Belize became an independent country. Today those once-primitive lodgings are the oldest five-star hotel in Belize, Victoria House.

"We wanted to have an English name to our hotel, this having been a British colony" said Browne Rice, one of the original founders. He is sitting with Ab Fay, another of the original investors. The two men, who have been friends since childhood, own the hotel outright. Sitting in a quiet, comfortable room just off the bar, they remember how the whole thing came about.

By the late 1970s both were successful businessmen. Mr. Fay was a developer, among other businesses, and Mr. Rice had quit his job as a stockbroker earlier in the decade and started a steak house in Houston that took off. He says it was a success because it appealed to "auto-part dealers and bank presidents." Both men had some spare cash when the Belize opportunity came along. The Ambergris Caye property was discovered by a home builder in Houston named Mervin Key. It was nine acres with six hundred feet of beachfront.

"It was for sale for $48,000, which was a pretty good bargain even then. He put a group of investors together, fourteen of us, and everybody put up $30,000," said Mr. Fay. The extra money was to develop the property, not an easy task. First, the land had to be cleared. That turned out to be the easy part.

Today Ambergris Caye is overflowing with development, with modern construction equipment making new condos and hotels a lot easier to build than almost forty years ago. For starters, there was no electricity at the site, less than two miles south of San Pedro, then a sleepy fishing village. For power they used two diesel generators they brought down from Houston. If a generator broke down, which happened often, there was no phoning for spare parts — there were no phones — and parts came from Houston.

One of the partners lived on site, looking forward to life in a tropical paradise.

"This guy's dream was to come down here and build a small hotel, bring his family, and live happily ever after. So he hired some contractors and we started building. It took two years to get to where there were a few tents and a dining room. The reason it took so long was back then there were no barges from the mainland. This island had twelve hundred people then; basically it was a little fishing village. We decided to build out of concrete and nobody else had done that here," said Browne Rice.

"We started construction during the rainy season and we couldn't do any logging so we opted for masonry material, but we found out you can't use this beach sand to make concrete with because it's coral sand. We had to import silica sand from the mainland by the boatload. Sailboats, with no motors, loaded with sand to the gunnels," recalled Mr. Fay.

"They would get as close as they could and then shovel the sand into a canoe, bring it to the beach then shovel it into a wheelbarrow then take the wheelbarrow up to the job site, which had a piece of plywood. They would put the sand on the plywood and throw a little cement in there, squirt it with water and stir it up and go to work. So, it was pretty labour-intensive, but labour was nothing back then."

The hotel didn't take off right away, and that's an understatement. For one thing, it wasn't that easy to get to Belize from the United States, and why would tourists come to a place they had never heard of?

"We opened up Victoria House without much fanfare at the time. Nobody showed up, nobody knew where Belize was. Back then you had to fly from New Orleans to Belize City on TACA Airlines," said Mr. Fay. "Small planes were just starting to fly out here to the island then, using little Cessna 180s and then 206s. Now they have a fleet of twelve Caravans, which is indicative of the growth of this island." The dream of the tropic idyll faded when things didn't go quite as planned. The home builder from Houston moved down to run the small hotel, but he had a weakness for rum.

"We were open for about a year and one of our friends from Houston came down here and he came back and said, 'You guys need to go down there and check on your hotel.' So I flew down here and our managing partner, like a lot of gringos who had moved down here, had fallen off into the rum bottle and was just drunk all the time."

The managing partner was out, though he continued to live in Belize, and the place was run by a competent local manager with Browne Rice overseeing things from his office in Houston, flying down once a month. Most of the partners started to panic.

"It was like owning a racehorse that didn't win: you have to feed the son of a bitch all the time," said Mr. Rice. "There were cash calls from the partners because we had to have money to make the payroll and stay in business. The cash calls turned out to be a godsend for Ab and me because all of the partners over the years got tired of putting money up. Some of them had never even been here."

They bought out the original partners for their initial investment and the two childhood friends ended up owning the hotel through San Pedro House Limited, doing business as Victoria House Hotel. Around 1985 business started to pick up. Soon there was a direct flight from Houston to Belize City, and that made it easier for both Americans and Canadians to get to Belize.

Fay and Rice were believers and started to expand, at first building rooms over the dining room. Back then there was a beautiful tree-lined road along the beach, and the hotel would pick up its guests at the airport in San Pedro with an old pickup truck that had wooden benches in the back, and take them along the beautiful sandy road to the hotel.

"I drove that truck down here from Houston. It was quite a trip through Mexico," said Mr. Fay. "It was a Chevrolet pickup truck. We built a little house on it and brought some scuba gear down here and some three-wheel motorcycles."

Looking at the verdant grounds of the Victoria House Hotel today, it is hard to believe it was once all sand; which was sometimes a problem because when a wind hit it could blow sand through the screens. There might be a layer of sand on the bedspreads when guests returned to their rooms.

Someone, probably the manager Fidel, had the idea to plant grass. Or at least he was convinced it was his idea, since he would have to tend to the grass and he had never met a lawn mower. The grass was planted, and next came the first gas-powered lawn mower in San Pedro.

About the same time the two men tired of running diesel generators for electricity, bit the bullet, and paid

$24,000 to connect to the power line in San Pedro, which by then was a little more than a mile from the hotel.

As the place filled with guests, people staying in the rooms above the bar would sometimes complain if there were rowdy parties below.

"So, in 1988, we built this bar out here and by then we needed more rooms so we built those two fourplexes, also in 1988. Obviously, we grew this out of our earnings over time," said Mr. Rice.

"My wife thought I was crazy coming down here, but I promised that our kids would still go to college," laughed Mr. Fay.

In the beginning the guests were scuba divers and, to a smaller degree, fishermen.

"Then there were people who just came for the adventure of a third-world country. Nobody had heard of it and they knew it was safe, English-speaking, and the government was stable, and you could buy land and own a free title to it, unlike a lot of other foreign countries," said Mr. Rice.

"Also, the laws here are based on English common law, which makes it easy to do business. So, those were the original tourists and they also came for this reef, the second longest reef in the world. As time went by, the mainland started to develop for tourists. There's a lot of stuff to do on the mainland: Mayan ruins, underground rivers, horseback riding in the mountains, and all kinds of stuff. So, as that grew it opened up a little wider audience for Belize and with the direct flights out of Houston, that helped a great deal. Now, of course, people come from all over the world. Most of our guests come from Texas and secondly from California, thirdly from New York and the East Coast, and fourthly from the U.K."

The longest either of them stays on the island is a month. The two friends have businesses together back in Texas. Theirs is a success story of how to do business in Belize, even if it isn't full time. Same way I do it.

These two men are true Texas gentlemen, who leap to their feet if a lady gets up in their presence, and great raconteurs. It is truly a pleasure to listen to the story of how they built this hotel to the success it is today. There was one funny anecdote they told us over dinner. One night an American woman and her daughter were visiting from San Pedro. It was late, and one of the gentleman-owners offered them a spare casita for the night. The two were also travelling with their dog, a giant Great Dane.

They checked at the desk and were told the room was empty. When the door opened, the first one in was the very friendly Great Dane, who leapt onto the bed, on top of a honeymooning couple. The woman screamed, and the man hid under the covers. There were no hard feelings; the honeymooning couple has been back to Victoria House since.

• • • • •

Mahogany Bay is a new development at the southern end of Ambergris Caye, just south of Victoria House. Beth Clifford is the developer and CEO of the project. An M.B.A. from Babson College, one of the top business schools in the United States, she worked on Wall Street, then at Digital Equipment Corporation, and ran a management consulting and software company in Silicon Valley for seventeen years. Ms. Clifford splits her time between Belize and her two houses in Maine.

Mahogany Bay.

Mahogany Bay at night.

She is the modern face of development in Belize. We spoke to her at her development office, beside the new sushi restaurant and across the street from the coffee shop in the micro-village she has created. She is an articulate woman, so I'll let her tell her story.

I came to Belize in 2002. We call ourselves emerging-market boutique developers so we want to be where the market is going. I had been developing in the United States and worked on a couple of projects in Cabo San Lucas, in Mexico. I researched Central America and the Caribbean for property; I was looking for the next emerging market in the Caribbean for the travel industry.

What interested me about Belize was its close proximity to the United States, English-speaking, stable currency as it's pegged to the U.S. dollar, and British Commonwealth laws. Also, relatively low land prices compared to the rest of the Caribbean.

We looked at all the Central American countries. Panama was already baked and not where we wanted to go: it was already a mature market. We looked at Costa Rica and thought it was also a mature market. We didn't really look at El Salvador or Honduras because of their crime issues and instability in the government.

We looked at Nicaragua but we didn't like the customer that was going there, which was the low-cost pensioner. People there are trying to retire on $10,000 a year and I don't want to build houses for those people. Then we looked at Guatemala, as well, but when we came to Belize we knew that this was it. This had all the right indicators to become the next Cabo San Lucas or the next Cancún.

We're modelled after Seaside and Rosemary Beach and those areas in the Florida panhandle. It's in what is known as the Redneck Riviera. It's called that. It was built in the 1980s and it was the flagship product that completely changed resort development with Seaside. Our planners were part of that: Rosemary Beach, Alys Beach — and those are products that started out at a quarter of a million in the 1980s and now it's three- to eight-million-dollar houses in the middle of nowhere in Florida. It's all about creating a community and creating value.

Mahogany Bay Village is made of three things:

Number one is a townlet, which is a village with retail, commercial, food and beverage, and services. We are also looking at integrating medical services, as well. The idea with the village is that we're 1.1 miles south of San Pedro Town and they're not making any more land there, so it really creates a complimentary town to downtown San Pedro. Downtown San Pedro is shabby-chic but it's an amenity and people come to go to downtown San Pedro. It has great food and beverage, it has great local flavour, and it has all that. So, it's how do you build a compliment to that when they are not making any more land downtown.

Two, we have the Hilton resort, where we have got the Curio Collection by Hilton, the hotel product. It is planned for 305 hotel rooms. So far, we have sold about 250 or 260 of them and we open this fall with the Curio.

Three, is our branded residential product under Coastal Living, which is a brand available through Time Incorporated, which is the largest media company in the United States. They have lifestyle magazines like *Coastal Living* and *Southern Living* and *Sunset.*

Our hotel product is a condo hotel product so it's owned by investors and put into the rental pool. Those properties start at $190,000 and go to $800,000 depending on the size of the properties or the number of units. We have a hotel management company who manages it. They hire all the professionals and managers to go and operate the hotel.

People started moving in in the summer of 2017 and the hotel opened in the fall. We did the first architectural drawings in March of 2013 and we did the first building, which is the one that says, "The Welcome Centre," over here in July of 2013 and since then we have built 300,000 square feet of product. So, we are the fastest-built project in the country of Belize.

This is the biggest and most aggressive project, which brought the first international high-end brand, which is the Hilton Curio, to the country of Belize. It's the fastest-selling project and the fastest-built project. All of our buildings are built out of Belizean hardwoods and softwoods.

We use mahogany, cabbage bark, Santa Maria, bullet tree and Caribbean pine. The first four are hardwoods. We make our houses in our factory in Belmopan and then ship them flat-packed to the island and then we erect them and finish them on the property. Our Coastal Living Lifestyle house, 2,400 square feet, was completely finished in seven weeks.

It sells in the mid-600s plus the pool. That product was in *Coastal Living* in their November issue. We are building houses in eight weeks

> versus eighteen months, which is the standard delivery time for a house in Belize. They are building out of concrete, which I can't say enough negative things about, so I won't.

John Turley, the number one real-estate salesperson in Belize, says Mahogany Bay is a game changer.

"I think that it is a turning point for all development on the island. There are a couple of things that will have a great effect on Ambergris Caye: The type of construction is one. That in and of itself is groundbreaking. The fact that it is a master-planned Caribbean village and is the first development with all underground utilities and the first development on this island to aspire to be a new downtown or a new San Pedro. It is not just a hotel but residential, commercial, and retail and restaurants and shops. Up until now most hotels on the island were five acres in size and placed anywhere. Mahogany Bay Village is the first hotel and/or resort on Ambergris Caye to bring a named brand or flag (hotel brand) to the market, which establishes credibility for other brands and flags," says Turley.

• • • • •

There are micro-businesses that flourish in Belize. Joyce Nsiah-Perovic is from Ghana, and lived and worked in Jamaica and Grand Cayman before coming to Belize in 2015. She owns and operates Polish, a salon in Mahogany Bay right next door to Beth Clifford's office and across the street from the coffee shop. It is as modern and sleek as a new iPhone. One spring afternoon she welcomes

Joyce Nsiah-Perovic caring for a customer in her salon.

Toshiya Tsujimoto.

Ab Fay from Victoria House across the way; he is in for a haircut. Next a Canadian visitor chats as she gets a mani-pedi. Joyce is an open, charming woman, and has the personality you need to succeed in this business. She is a perfect example of how someone can start a very small business and succeed in Belize.

Toshiya Tsujimoto runs the JYOTO, one of only two sushi restaurants in Belize, and in my view the best, in fact one of the best anywhere. Toshiya is a master and comes up with the unusual, not just the cookie-cutter sushi you see everywhere. This is yet another example of a young person starting a successful business from scratch in Belize.

JYOTO is in Mahogany Bay's micro-town, still in San Pedro, but a fifteen-minute cab ride or golf-cart trek from the main town.

"I love cooking with local ingredients, seafood, in the Japanese way. People love it. It is easy to get the raw materials here, so the sushi is the best it can be," says Toshiya, who has become a friend of mine; after all, I was born in Japan too.

Toshiya came to Belize in September of 2016. He left Japan when he was twenty and perfected his knowledge of sushi in San Francisco, where he worked for seven years. He worked as a sushi chef for a couple of years in Malta, the small island nation in the Mediterranean. He has worked as a sushi chef in more than a dozen countries. Then he read about Belize.

"I had never heard of Belize before and I thought I should go there. So I came here and found it beautiful. I researched and I met the people in Mahogany Bay Village," says Toshiya. "Not only am I the only sushi chef on Ambergris Caye, I am the only Japanese person on the island."

Toshiya is a partner in the restaurant, and he has a Japanese investor helping him — the same person who owned and operated the sushi restaurant in Malta.

There are 128 seats in his restaurant and it is popular. The biggest reason for its success is the skill and passion of the young chef (he turns thirty-five in 2018).

"First, I love the ingredients and they are easy to get and very fresh. Next to the ocean, same as Japan. Also, it's close to the mainland where you can get the vegetables, fruits, and spices. It's all delivered by Tropic Air so easily and much cheaper than in other countries," says Toshiya.

"We see many Canadians and Americans here and they know about sushi and Japanese food and they can pay for the quality food. So there are customers and there's fish but just no chef, right? So, I'm the chef here so I'm confident. It's very simple."

A unique Belize success story.

Art in Belize: A Unique Way of Discovering the Culture and How to Do Business

Lindsey Hackston operates the Belizean Arts gallery in the centre of San Pedro, just a few steps from the beach. She represents artists from Ambergris Caye, the mainland of Belize, and the other cayes. She opened her gallery around 1989, and not only runs a successful business, but nurtures the careers of Belizean artists.

"Ninety-five percent of the artists we represent come from Belize, but we do have some that are connected with Belize, but don't live here," says Ms. Hackston. Some of these artists have exhibited outside Belize, but she says most of them want to stay here.

The people browsing through Lindsey Hackston's gallery reflect the diverse base of people visiting Belize.

Lindsey Hackston in her San Pedro art gallery.

She is an excellent barometer of how that base is changing, and her customers are richer than the average.

"Most of our customers are Canadians or Americans but we get a few Europeans, particularly in the summer, and now we are getting occasionally some people from South and Central America. They've got [an airline] connection with Panama now and we are getting some people from Argentina occasionally, and some Mexicans, too. Even though we're on the border with Mexico we never used to get them travelling here, but there are more coming."

The artists mirror the ethnic diversity of rainbow Belize: Pen Cayetano is Garifuna, Nelson Young is Creole from Caye Caulker, and Jorge Castianis and Eduardo Alamea are Hispanic from Ambergris Caye. There are up-and-coming artists such as Carlos Linarez, Leo Vasquez, and Careo who are doing interesting work.

All of the local artists are self-taught; some produce fascinating primitive art, others more conventional pieces, but all reflect the unique nature of Belize. Some of them have shown their art outside Belize but in general they aren't really known; they have done shows but some of them don't really want to leave and become famous; they want to stay right here. The art at this and other galleries is truly unique and acts a reminder of the beauty and culture of Belize, whether you hang it in your place in Belize or back at home.

There are art galleries in almost every corner of Belize, some of them doubling as souvenir shops. According to a YouTube documentary on art in Belize, three of the most important are in San Pedro. When Lindsey Hackston started her art gallery, it was the first in Belize, and only sixteen feet square. It is much larger today.

Jerry Lansing, another expat, operates the Gallery of San Pedro, which started as a hammock shop but expanded into arts. Paintings hang on racks. "We have a unique way of displaying," he says. "You can shop just like you are shopping for clothes. We keep just the raw canvas, because 90 percent of our customers are tourists, so this way we can just roll the artworks up and put them in a tube.

"There a few people who are really interested in the art and they love it and we get browsers who pick up jewellery and that sort of thing and that helps. We have to sell a few other things to be able to display art. If we relied 100 percent on paintings, we'd be closed. So, we have some beautiful jewellery and crafts that are all handmade."

Lindsey Hackston is a soft-spoken woman, but beneath her gentle manner is a keen observer of the local scene and how newcomers adjust to life in Belize. People who come to Belize are mesmerized by the place, but she lives the reality. As someone who has lived and run a business in Belize, Ms. Hackston has advice for people who want to open a business in the country. In short, don't expect things to work the same way they do back home.

"I think a lot of people come here and they are mesmerized by the sea and the beautiful colours, the light and the really fun, smiling, friendly people," says Ms. Hackston. "But then when they actually come to live here they have to realize that even with a very different culture and even though people speak English, they do things and think quite differently. The longer you stay here the more you understand that. So, if you have the view that you're going to enjoy the differences, it can be great. I find it fascinating. But if you want things to be the way they are at home, you're just going to get really frustrated in so many different ways. One of the expat cries often is: 'Well, in America or England, we do it this way.' It's kind of irrelevant and you have to forget that."

She says it is different if you are coming to Belize to retire.

"When you come down here financially equipped, everybody is very happy to help you.

"Then there are some expats like myself who have created businesses that have actually been of great benefit to locals because, with the art, nobody else was doing it. I feel I've contributed a lot in the arts and crafts side of Belize, but competition is quite painful here. I think it's nice, if you're an expat, to come down and do something that's going to benefit the community," she says.

Ms. Hackston says there are ways of doing business that would shock someone in Britain or the U.S., but she accepts them. One example is that artists sometimes deliver their art to her at odd hours, even tossing a rolled-up canvas over the fence at her house. She is cool with that. She has noticed a marked increase in tourism over the past few years, and she feels new resorts provide much-needed work for the local population.

"For people like snorkellers, obviously the reef is the main draw; but a lot of our repeat visitors come here because they like the laid-back atmosphere; it's not Cancún. You're still mixing with the locals, it's not just tourists; you can sit down at a bar and there's a local sitting next to you."

Jeremy Meighan, Wyndham Grand: From Wall Street to Ambergris Caye

Jeremy Meighan is developing the luxury Wyndham Hotel on the booming north end of Ambergris Caye. The site is spectacular, on the water facing the barrier reef. Guests will have a show every night, with the surf lighting up as it crashes into the reef.

Jeremy is a dual citizen, American and Belizean; both his parents were born in Belize and lived at 22 Barrack Road in Belize City. His father, Danny Meighan, was a city councillor in Belize City before moving to the United States in 1978 when Jeremy was five years old.

"I spent most of my childhood going back to Belize in summers and at Christmas whenever I was able to. I think it was a well-thought-out plan by my parents to make sure that I always kept my culture and as I continued to grow I always had Belize on my mind," says Jeremy.

He had a successful career on Wall Street and is now giving back to the country where he was born, bringing the Wyndham brand to Belize. He calls it "approachable luxury," meaning it is not priced into the stratosphere.

"It is a Wyndham Grand, the highest brand that they have within their portfolio, the first five-star major-flagged hotel to come to Belize. We're working as smart and as fast as we can to finish it by December 2018," says Jeremy, who is a partner and owner.

"I think we fit very well into the demographic of travellers right now. We are starting to see a lot of luxury travellers coming to Belize, and we don't believe we have enough supply for that segment of the market. It's a great market to build into."

Jeremy thinks Belize offers a unique experience that can't really be compared to other Caribbean resorts or those in Mexico. "I think we are unique on our own and I think that is what will sell us in the future as being a top tourist destination."

The huge growth in the number of flights into Belize is one of the reasons Jeremy and the Wyndham are building in Ambergris Caye.

"I am excited to see the air traffic that's coming to Belize. The [arrival of] the Southwests and JetBlues of the world along with WestJet lowers the prices by getting some competition into the market, and it will allow the prices to normalize," he says.

One of the possibilities that really excites Jeremy Meighan is the prospect of an airport at the north end of Ambergris Caye. The Wyndham will be successful without that, but will boom with it.

CHAPTER 5

OTHER ENTREPRENEURS

JOHN Turley is a titan of real estate, not just in Belize, but in all of Central America, and the CEO and co-owner of RE/MAX for the Caribbean and Central America region, which takes in thirty-five islands, countries, and territories. That includes Barbados, the Lesser Antilles, Jamaica, the Cayman Islands, and the Bahamas: basically all of the Caribbean except Cuba and the Dominican Republic.

"I took over as CEO in January of 2015 and in the ensuing years we have grown from fifty-two offices to seventy, and from 225 agents to over 420 agents. This growth is indicative of the massive growth that is taking place throughout the Caribbean Central America Region."

John has the opportunity to live in any of the places that people from the north are dreaming of, but he chose Belize.

"I moved here for quality of life twelve years ago with my wife and three children. We had set out to determine where the best place would be to raise our children and the quality of life. It just so happened that the markers and indicators for quality of life for us as a family happened to coincide with the critical drivers as to why people choose to be tourists and relocate here as expats in retirement. What started as a quality-of-life proposition quickly turned into an investment opportunity," says John.

Turley is an American who had experience as a real-estate investor before moving to Ambergris Caye. From his base in San Pedro he works as an active broker, in addition to running the string of RE/MAX outlets. John has been the number one agent for RE/MAX for the Caribbean and Latin America region for six straight years. "I finished top three in the world out of 110,000 [RE/MAX] agents based purely on sales, in an island of twenty-two thousand people, which is indicative of just how much is happening in this market," says John.

"The thing that is unique about Belize is that not only are we going through an explosive growth in tourism, with Belize having become recognized as a major tourist destination, but we have a distinct advantage when it comes to the baby boomers and the exodus of people from the United States and Canada to warmer climates," says John. "Belize has the distinction of being the only English-speaking country in Central America. *International Living* magazine cited Belize as the top English-speaking destination in the Caribbean. With Americans, 91 percent only speak English, so, being an English-speaking destination, there is a far greater comfort level."

Belize's number one real-estate agent says the type of person moving to Belize is changing. He says the growth in both tourism and the real-estate market is coming in the mid to high end of the market.

"The resorts that have the highest occupancy and the areas where you see the greatest demand are those that have the highest average daily rate. Likewise, with condo development, developers are not adding any inventory at the low or middle end of the market, they are adding the mid to high range," says John. "Within condo developments, for example, the first units to sell out are the larger, more expensive units. Penthouses are always the first to go, almost regardless of the price. So we're seeing the million-dollar-plus category, rather than being the exception to the rule, is really at the forefront of where the demand is. The first million-dollar condo sale in Ambergris Caye was in July of 2011 was at Grand Caribe. It was a four-bedroom, four-bath penthouse, 3,600 square feet for 1.1 million. That was the sound barrier of the million-dollar condo sales. This last weekend at a development here on the island called La Sirene, I brokered a three-million-dollar penthouse sale, which was the first three-million-dollar condo sale on Ambergris Caye and, ironically, that happens to be the starting price for a three-bedroom condo on the seven-mile beach in Grand Cayman. So we have a long way to go to beat Grand Cayman but I think that is the market we most closely emulate here in Ambergris Caye."

Ambergris Caye and Grand Cayman are about the same size, though the Caymans are more advanced in infrastructure and development. The population of Grand Cayman is 65,000, while Ambergris Caye is around 25,000. Turley says there is a lot of infrastructure work that has to be done; the mayor of Ambergris Caye, who calls his island the economic engine of the whole country, is pushing for it.

The expansion of the Belize international air terminal, and more flights coming into the country, is driving growth, says John Turley. He gives just one example:

"As of June 4, 2017, Southwest Airlines started direct, non-stop service from Fort Lauderdale, which adds 1,160 passenger seats per week to an already busy international airport."

A man who has statistics at his fingertips, Turley says Canadians represented 5.3 percent of the overall tourism arrivals at Belize international airport before WestJet started flying in from Toronto and Calgary. Air Canada is now in the mix.

"You now have one sixth of the Canadian population having direct flight access to Belize. I would argue that the impact of direct flights from Canada is disproportionately higher than the impact from within the U.S. because of the British Commonwealth ties between Canada and Belize, and the fact that so many Canadians are looking to get out of Canada in the winter months," says Turley.

Though he lives and works in Ambergris Caye, John Turley and his agents cover the whole country. He describes Placencia as a beautiful location. "It's probably the closest thing we have to Vancouver when you think of having proximity to the water with mountain views. But the real up-and-coming story for Belize is Caye Caulker, surpassing Placencia as the number two tourism destination," says Turley. He says many people were surprised that Caye Caulker moved up so suddenly.

One reason is that Caye Caulker became more affordable. Another is that the type of person going there changed, as we describe in some detail elsewhere in this book.

"You still have the backpackers and what I'll call the 'hostel' crowd, and, for Europeans, it's particularly appealing. If you compare it to Playa del Carmen, Mexico, for example, you have a large influx of Europeans. Caye Caulker more closely emulates the demographic of a

Marie Sharp

Some of hottest hot sauce in the world comes from Belize. Marie Sharp's hot sauce is a blend of carrots, vinegar, and onions with the heat coming from crushed habañeros. If she wants to turn up the heat, she adds more habañero.

Marie Sharp started her company in 1981 at the family farm in Dangriga. She is truly a homegrown Belize success story. She still owns the company and the factory that produces a whole line of hot sauces, with names like Marie Sharp's Belizean Heat or Marie Sharp's Beware: Comatose Heat Level.

Marie Sharp was born in Belize City in 1940. She is a well-educated woman and taught school for a while before becoming an executive secretary at the Citrus Company of Belize. In her spare time, she grew habañero peppers and used those she didn't sell to make a homemade hot sauce. To make a hot story short, that sauce is sold today all over the world. Google "Marie Sharp," and up pop links to Amazon and shops around the world.

Marie Sharp is in the Hot Sauce Hall of Fame. It's an award given at the Hot Sauce Expo held annually in New York City. She still works at the company she started, as do several of her children.

Playa del Carmen with a much greater European influence than we see here even in Ambergris Caye. So property values have increased. Caye Caulker is home to a lot of eclectic, funky boutique hotels, shops, and restaurants. There are some phenomenal restaurants there now."

• • • • •

Simon Reardon-Smith owns and operates eleven duty-free shops in Belize. His company services airports and the cruise ship terminal, where most people buy local rum and tobacco — but the most lucrative shops are at the borders with Mexico and Guatemala, where people from those countries buy whisky and cheap cigarettes.

Reardon-Smith came to Belize with the British Army. He was a captain with the Queen's Dragoon Guards and was commander of the armoured Caribbean group; tanks that patrolled the border with Guatemala, which, along with a fleet of Harrier jets, kept Belize safe from any encroachments from Guatemala. "We patrolled the Guatemala border and it was very effective." Twelve years ago Reardon-Smith fell in love with a woman from Belize and is now married with two children. He lives just outside Belize City and has a beach house in Caye Caulker.

"Belize has been good to me," he says. "This is a pretty free country and it is absolutely gorgeous. There is not the regulation you find in Europe, the U.S., and Canada. There is lots of potential here, in particular with the borders with Mexico and Guatemala."

• • • • •

Real-estate broker Dmitri Ioudine moved from Moscow to Canada after the breakup of the old Soviet Union, then discovered Belize. He lives in San Pedro and Canada.

> I've shopped around. I felt very comfortable investing here, because it is a British Commonwealth country, people speak English, all the contracts are in English, and you can trust the land-transfer system. It's a very transparent process, just like Canada and the U.S. You put in an offer, you get a contract, you get a lawyer, then you have your title. It's very straightforward, as opposed to nearby countries where

> there are restrictions on foreigners owning property and all the contracts are in Spanish. It's a big gamble buying property in many of those places.

• • • • •

The people who've moved to Belize tend to be adventurous, and that is one of the things that makes the place so interesting.

Carlos Utrera took a roundabout way to get to Belize. The well-educated Cuban, now in his early forties, left the island and ended up in the United States. A born entrepreneur, he bought part of a small cable-TV-installation business in Philadelphia. But the northern winters were a bit much for someone used to the warmth of Havana, so he has run a couple of businesses in San Pedro. He enjoys the laid-back lifestyle of Ambergris Caye, but running a business keeps his mind sharp.

One of my business associates is also a permanent resident of Belize. He was born on a farm in Saskatchewan and has a couple of university degrees including an M.B.A. from the Richard Ivey School of Business at the University of Western Ontario. After working in commercial real estate in Western Canada, he came to Belize. You might think Belize is a bit sleepy for an entrepreneur to live here full time, but he keeps busy with real-estate deals and the details of development.

He has a wide range of business interests and is a thoroughly modern businessman, connected to the world with high-speed internet and to the rest of Belize by our rather efficient local commuter airlines, Tropic Air and Maya Island Air.

• • • • •

There is a small but growing community of modern business types that call Belize home, either full-time or part-time. One of the things I have noticed is that local business people learn from these hyper-connected people, like Mahogany Bay's Beth Clifford or RE/MAX's John Turley, and they in turn learn the more relaxed and civilized way of doing business in Belize.

CHAPTER 6

WHAT MAKES ME TICK

JUST being in Belize makes me a little more introspective than most entrepreneurs. Outside my little paradise I tend to have what I call a Type Triple-A personality. But a few days here has me thinking about who I really am.

Sikhs are known for their warrior tradition, cultivated in their self-defence and safeguarding of the Khyber Pass. When this is passed down through the generations, you develop a survival instinct, as I have.

When asked my religion, I say that I am Sikh; however, I would say I am more spiritual than religious, as I am non-practicing. That said, despite orthodox first impressions, Sikhism is, in fact, a very liberal culture. You go to a Sikh temple and they sing songs like the southern Baptists and invite you in for a meal. Sikhs have fitted well into Canada, though it hasn't been easy. When the Royal Canadian Legion wouldn't allow turbaned Sikhs into their halls, they didn't realize that we've won more Victoria Crosses than any other group. In fact, Sir John A. Macdonald once suggested bringing in a Sikh battalion to protect Canada from the Americans.

Our family's migration to Canada started when my grandfather, as a teenager, moved from Punjab to Hong

Kong. He eventually became a trader and established the North China Shipping Company, which exported goods to Japan, where I was born in 1965. Six years later our family moved to Liberia to tap the trading market of West Africa, but was displaced by civil war. We lost everything, packed up yet again, and arrived in Vancouver.

Eventually our family moved to Calgary, where at first we faced prejudice: racial slurs, harassment, and bullying. My mother was fired from her job at the post office strictly because of its racist attitude. But we didn't become bitter; rather, we used the court system and fought the case with the Crown corporation, and won. She was reinstated in her job a year later.

It was tough for me to get a job in Calgary. Thankfully, that wouldn't be true today, but twenty-five years ago it was a very different climate. There were only stereotyped positions available to Sikhs, and it was really hard to break in. For example, we were banned from well-paying office jobs, and no oil companies would hire me.

If people won't give you a job, you make your own, and that's what I did. In 1984, at age nineteen, I bought two houses, fixed them up, and sold them for an $18,000 profit. For the next fifteen years I bought and sold Calgary real estate worth about $150 million. I worked out of the trunk of my car, armed with a cell-phone. What drove me to work seventy hours a week or more was that my family had lost everything in Liberia after the coup, and I vowed it would never happen again.

Along the way I realized that I didn't know everything. So at the age of thirty-two I spent two years at Canada's top business school, the University of Western Ontario's Richard Ivey School of Business. In May of my

Bob Dhillon in front of his Mainstreet office.

first year, I incorporated Mainstreet Equity Corporation as a numbered Alberta company. It became my main investment vehicle.

I used every available course at Ivey to formulate the strategy for Mainstreet. Whether it was building a brand, running an efficient operation, financing growth, or making a speech, I thought about the lessons in terms of what they meant for my company.

After I graduated I took the company public. The people I had met showed me that building wealth, and holding on to it, needed a different strategy than being a super-successful real-estate flipper. I started buying properties to hold and moved into a permanent office in one of my buildings.

Along the way I have learned to recognize opportunity where others see failure. Here's an example. Calgary's Forest Lawn district had sixty deserted cars and trucks in its derelict parking lot, holes in living-room walls, and all the telltale signs of having been a druggie hangout. I invested $2.3 million, doubled the rents, and turned a slum into a middle-class complex.

When it comes to real estate I look out for the details and watch every penny. Replacing toilets with modern, low-volume fixtures, for example, reduces water consumption from 6 gallons per flush to 1.6; substituting sixty-watt light bulbs with twenty-dollar fluorescent lights reduces annual electricity consumption from thirty dollars to eight dollars.

Today, Mainstreet occupies a unique niche, between the small landlords at the bottom and the giant property holders such as Trizec and Brookfield at the top. What I specialize in is multi-family, mid-tiered residential rental properties. I started in Alberta, moved west to Vancouver, and east into Saskatchewan. Mainstreet now owns almost 11,000 rental units in Western Canada.

I am proud that I built a billion-dollar company after starting with nothing. Here are the four things I keep at the forefront of my thinking:

1. Counter-cyclical thinking. Buy when others are selling. We did that in a recent real-estate sell-off.
2. Adding value.
3. Geographic targeting. Not all locations are created equal.
4. Get there before everybody else.

Now, as I've outlined throughout this book, I am involved not just in my Canadian real-estate holdings, but in Belize, as well. The country and I seemed to discover each other at the right moment. It was an English-speaking democracy with little extreme poverty, and still virgin tourist territory. With only 360,000 people, it has all the advantages for expats: banks protected by privacy laws, a diving paradise, dozens of Mayan ruin sites, and 540 species of wild birds.

I bought a 2,700-acre island and marketed beach lots, only a few with price tags of under $1 million. There are a few Hollywood types who own beachfront estates nearby. This property in Belize will be the next St. Barts, but without the hedonistic crowds and with a relaxed style. It has the best fishing, diving, sailing, and white sand beaches, and the kind of lifestyle we all dream about.

When I look back, I realize I owe my success to Canada. If I hadn't moved to Calgary, I wouldn't have had one-tenth of the success anywhere else in the world. I owe my start to Alberta, because it was not a closed shop. If you create a business model there that has a success pattern, you can branch out to other parts of Canada.

My Real-Estate Formula

The secret to my Canadian real-estate success is simple: I buy distressed mid-market properties that are in foreclosure or in rough shape and fit what I call my value chain model. In simple terms it means that in every part of the business chain you make things better, or add value. In almost all small family-owned apartment complexes there is an abysmal level of quality. There is poor service for the tenants, from windows that don't work to leaky faucets. I take over the buildings, bring them up to our standard, which is the same standard that middle-class renters are looking for, and at the same time increase revenues 40 percent.

Mainstreet focuses on mid-market apartments. The large investors ignore these properties, even though they are 65 percent of the market. The type of buildings we buy are almost always owned by mom-and-pop operators, who have, in many cases, neglected them for as long as thirty-five years. In many places, rent control has seen to that. If owners can't increase rents, they give up on improving their properties.

The other part of my real-estate life is in Belize. It is, of course, totally different: in Belize we are starting from scratch, building houses and condominiums on Costa del Sol. There are ways my main business correlates with what I do in Belize: first is finding value. The reason I am in the multi-family game in Canada is because the opportunity exists. To put it simply, I could have gone to St. Barts, say, but there's no opportunity remaining there.

The second is timing. This is a great time to be in the rental-apartment business in Canada. It has been ignored for decades, while the demand is there. The same is true with Belize. While the so-called smart money was busy shoehorning development into Cancún or building cheek by jowl in Barbados and St. Barts, Belize has remained an almost untouched paradise. And it will stay that way because the government and people like me, who are actively developing it, want to keep it that way.

Opportunity exists in Belize, pure and simple, and that is why it fits in with my real-estate formula and business philosophy. Also, there is perhaps more opportunity in a place like Belize than even in the booming cities of Western Canada. One reason is demand for waterfront vacation properties.

You have to ask yourself, with a growing population of people looking for these types of properties, is there a cap on the appreciation of waterfront real estate? The answer is obvious. Let's face it: apartment buildings have a limit on growth. If there is a 5 percent return on your investment, it will take a while before you see your investment double. But waterfront real estate could go up much more, as it has in other places in the Caribbean. It's conceivable that waterfront real estate in a place like Belize could quadruple in value. Of course I'm not making any promises, but just look at what happened in Barbados or the Caymans.

Belize is more than dollars and cents for me, though. It is also romance, and when you can combine that with opportunity, could life be any better?

PART III

THE PROMISE OF BELIZE

CHAPTER 7

THE ANATOMY OF PARADISE

WE are starting to see one of the biggest wealth transfers in history: approximately 75 million baby boomers will inherit money and property worth anywhere from $200,000 to $20 million or more from their parents. This is in addition to their own earnings and retirement savings.

This rich, aging demographic will drive growth in Belize. As people have seen their investments shrink, they want to put them someplace where they can be safe and sheltered. They also want to have some fun with their money. A beach house in Belize is a lot more enjoyable than a T-bill. Smart countries are thinking about how to capture that wealth. There are many ways to do it.

Baby boomers can expect to live longer and healthier lives than previous generations. "In America today a 70-year-old man has [just] a 2% chance of dying within a year; in 1940 this milestone was passed at 56," noted *The Economist* in a 2017 special report called "The New Old." It continued: "In 1950 just 5% of the world's population was over 65; in 2015 the share was 8%."

Longevity gains are huge. When Bismarck brought in the first old-age pension, for sixty-five-year-olds, the average life expectancy in Germany was forty-five. Today 90 percent of people in the rich world can expect to live to sixty-five.

Fewer see retirement as putting their feet up. "In America, those between 55 and 65 are now 65% more likely to start up companies than those between 20 and 34," said the report.

That means many will be coming to a tropical paradise like Belize to become self-employed, rather than working in the cold north. The retirement and business rules in Belize make it that much more attractive than other destinations.

Belize is promoting private health clinics for rich visitors. For example, private clinics attract talented doctors from other countries and they specialize in things such as knee operations that would cost Americans a fortune at home. The government doesn't plan these clinics, but Belize is making it easy for this type of innovation to flourish. Of course, this is coupled with a tax system for retirees that doesn't rob people of their savings.

One look at the following list tells you that Belize is a place where people are going to want to invest, work, and retire. It is a country that has it all.

My Top Twelve Reasons to Live and Invest in Belize

1. Freehold title to property: land title system similar to that used in the U.S. and Canada.
2. Right to vote for retirees.
3. No capital gains tax.
4. Ownership rights through Belize corporations.
5. Banking privacy laws: shelter your money legally.

6. English-speaking country.
7. Location: a two-hour flight from Miami, Atlanta, Houston, or Charlotte.
8. Low cost of living for tourists and retired people.
9. No taxes for retirees.
10. Easy rules for retirees to move to and live in Belize.
11. Spectacular natural beauty, tropical weather, and no crowds.
12. Ground zero for investment; prices cheap compared to other tropical waterfront getaways.

Belize can do all this because it is a place where the government makes the rules and then sits back and watches the growth. Local politicians realize that making it easier for entrepreneurs to operate will help provide employment for people in Belize and increase its tax base. You see this in the lack of bureaucratic and governmental interference.

One high-ranking official in the Belize government gave his version and the reason for bringing in such rules: "We have fiscal incentives law to encourage development. If you have a good project, you can get a tax exemption for five years. You can also get a duty-free exemption for bringing equipment into the country and that can be for as long as ten years. We see Belize developing without getting into heavy industrialization. We would like to blend the efficient growth we've seen in Singapore and the environmental beauty we see in Switzerland. We have a greater resource base than Singapore and we're nowhere near them. In this region we saw Costa Rica … and they have succeeded in convincing the world they are environmental purists."

Beltraide

Beltraide is the acronym for the Belize Trade and Investment Development Service. It is a government agency set up to encourage investment. To my mind it shows the government is keen on investment and making it easy to do business here. Here is an introduction to the agency:

> Apart from having the largest living Barrier Reef in the Western Hemisphere, Belize also provides the most dynamic and conducive business environment for both locals and foreigners. As a means to connect Belize to the rest of the world, Belize Trade and Investment Development Service (BELTRAIDE), has been charged with the task of doing so. Beltraide, a statutory body of the Government of Belize, is keen on attracting highly qualified investments, developing small and medium enterprises, as well as, promoting our "Made in Belize" products.

Beltraide should be the first stop for a prospective entrepreneur. Just Google *Beltraide* and all will be revealed.

Belize also has some of the region's most lenient residency laws for people from Canada, the United States, and Britain. You can declare permanent residency after you live in the country for one year. After that you have to spend one month a year in the country to maintain your residency status.

International Living rates Belize as the seventh-best place in the world to buy a second home. A free-market economy makes it even more enticing: a quiet haven where the rules favour the newcomers and where it is still cheap to buy property and development is still at the ground floor. Safe, affordable, and cheap.

The Last Virgin Paradise

Belize works. Parliamentary democracy and an open economy, among other factors, have come together to present a unique opportunity for people seeking paradise. Other Latin American countries should be taking off, but they are not; there is still a mistrust of what has proven to be the greatest economic driver in the world: free enterprise. The richest countries in the world are all liberal democracies, from the United States and the European Union to Canada and Finland. But the reality is the market economies are still richer and will be even more so when the smoke clears. Belize is far from rich, but in my view it is on the right track to prosperity. Politicians on both the government and opposition side understand this.

"You can't fight poverty without creating wealth," said a prominent retired politician from Belize. Many people don't understand why some countries make it and others don't. It's the little things that do them in, such as petty rules, corruption, and stifling bureaucracy. The Peruvian economist Hernando de Soto discusses this in his book *The Mystery of Capital: Why Capitalism Triumphs in the West and Fails Everywhere Else*. After reading this you realize that Belize has things right in the area of attracting investment and protecting private property.

De Soto uses many examples of countries getting things wrong, from Latin America to Africa. One of his favourites is Egypt, where the economy is in chaos. Like so many other countries in the world, says de Soto, Egypt has wealth but its riches remain locked because its people can't do simple things such as nail down the title to houses to live in or own the land they work.

"Most of the poor already possess the assets they need to make a success of capitalism. Even in the poorest countries, the poor save. The value of savings among the poor is, in fact, immense," he writes. "In Egypt, for instance, the wealth that the poor have accumulated is worth fifty-five times as much as the sum of all direct foreign investment ever recorded there, including the Suez Canal and the Aswan Dam." Yet without title to their land, and courts to enforce the rule of law, the poor can't use their assets to borrow and finance businesses. And he wrote that before the upheaval in Egypt that toppled Hosni Mubarak.

This is something I know about first-hand. My family came to Canada as economic refugees from West Africa, a region that is perhaps the most desperate example of economic and political failure in the world. Along with not having the right to own property, another huge problem in many parts of the world are the rules for starting a business. When I started my first business in Canada almost thirty years ago, it took just fifteen minutes and fifty dollars to register its name and receive the paper that allowed me to open a business bank account. I was nineteen years old. Everything was done in a morning. These days it is even faster: you can register a business online.

Later, when my business expanded, it was a simple thing to incorporate. It didn't take much time and cost less than $1,000. Try doing that in Peru or Egypt. Registering a business could take two years or more. Bank loans are unheard of for small businesses.

Although not rich by North American or European standards, the people of Belize are 50 percent richer than their neighbours in Honduras and a bit richer than those in Guatemala. Both those countries have political and social problems that don't exist in Belize. It has potential that other countries in the region can't touch. A complex set of circumstances has come together to make Belize the last virgin paradise in the Western world. This is a place that is two hours from the richest country in the world, and when Americans really discover it, they'll want a piece of paradise.

CHAPTER 8

FREEDOM — PERSONAL AND FISCAL

FOR many people freedom is an abstract idea; a word that has lost its meaning. Not for me. My family searched for freedom for three generations and we finally found it in Canada. Now I have discovered it again in Belize, my home away from home.

My grandfather left his Sikh homeland of the Punjab when he was sixteen. Like so many other of his countrymen, he sought better opportunities in the wider world. We come from the line of Sikhs who combine warrior and commercial cultures, guarding the fabled North-West Frontier and its trade routes into India. For centuries, Sikhs guarded the foothills of the Khyber Pass, beating off the invaders who came from the north.

The first stop was Hong Kong, where my grandfather, Saproon Singh Dhillon, became a trader and established the North China Shipping Company, which exported goods to Japan. I was born in Japan and still speak the language. When I was six years old, we moved to Liberia in West Africa, where the opportunities for a trading family seemed great. But civil war stripped Liberia of what freedom it had. In financial ruin, our family sought refuge in Vancouver.

There was freedom in Canada, but I sometimes wondered about tolerance. As a Sikh, I was taunted when I was growing up and called "Paki" on the way to school. Much of that base racism has disappeared over the years, but the combination of freedom and tolerance was one of the things that first impressed me about Belize.

It's the nature of Belize that makes it so tolerant and unique. As we discuss in detail elsewhere in this book, Belize was almost an accident in that it brought together so many different races and cultures while remaining apart from Spanish America. From the British buccaneers to the West India troops from Jamaica who settled here, mixing with the original Mayan inhabitants, it produced the rainbow hues of Belize that you see today. There are still new immigrants. Canadian Mennonites moved here in the twentieth century in search of tolerance and the freedom to be left alone. Now there is a growing colony of expats from all over the world. Along with retirees from the United States and Canada, there are people from Britain, Belgium, Holland, and Germany who come to Belize not just because of its spectacular beaches and geography, but because this is an oasis of tolerance.

Tolerance also extends to your money. All the government of Belize wants to know is that you have enough money to live on. That means documenting pension or investment income of US$2,000 a month. As *International Living* pointed out, that's enough money to live well. The magazine profiled an American couple who retired to Belize and kept expenses down by using solar power for their electricity and living on inexpensive locally grown food.

Once you have declared permanent residency (see page 92), you can maintain it by spending just one month of the year in the country. Now that's the kind of tolerance a lot of us can live with.

You'll Never Be Able to Vote in Mexico

Belize is so open to foreigners that they can easily acquire voting rights, either through the retirement program or by arranging to become permanent residents. If you come from a country in the Commonwealth, you can vote in the general election, which chooses the country's parliament and government.

Things can only get better with the openness of the current residents combined with the fresh ideas and wealth of the newcomers.

Remember: you'll never be able to vote in Mexico if you move there, and if you're a Canadian, you'll never have the right to vote for state politicians who tax snowbirds in Florida, Arizona, or Hawaii. Commonwealth citizens can vote in Belize (see below).

Belize doesn't place restrictions on the length of your stay. Once you've arranged your residency status, you can spend all year in Belize if you want.

From the Constitution of Belize

92. At any general election —

(a) every citizen of Belize or a citizen of any Commonwealth Country who has attained the age of eighteen years and who satisfies the requirement of the Representation of the People Act should have the right to vote.

Politics

Barack Obama was elected the first black president of the United States in 2008, the same year that Belize elected its first black prime minister, Dean Barrow. Belize is so different from its neighbours. For one thing there is no one ethnic hierarchy or old boys' network. The population is split into five or six ethnic groups and none of them is dominant. The people of Belize are descendants of Mayas and Africans, Carib Indians mixed with African slaves, Spanish settlers, and Scottish immigrants. Today you will also see people from India and China here. You sense the tolerance as soon as you arrive. There is no ethnic tension and no one group looks down on any other.

As the travel writer Joshua Berman quipped in his Moon Handbook *Belize*, "The extraordinary diversity of Belize's relatively tiny population … is similar to the rainbow of skin colors one finds in a New York City subway car — except in Belize, they're all making direct eye contact and talking and laughing with each other."

There are political differences, as there are in any democracy, but no matter which party is in power, the country continues on an even keel. There is as free and as highly opinionated a press in Belize as there is in any English-speaking country in the world. There are a surprising number of newspapers and media outlets, many of them expressing strong partisan opinions, but all of them managing to keep the politicians on their toes, which is their job in a free society.

• • • • •

Belize models its government on the British parliamentary system. There are two houses: the House of Representatives and the Senate. The House of Representatives has thirty-one constituencies, each of which elects a Member of Parliament for a five-year term. The electoral boundaries are redrawn by an independent commission that tries to keep the population of each district equal. Senators are appointed, though there is some democracy to the process, since senators are chosen by several groups: the ruling party, the opposition party, the church, business, unions, and NGOs.

The head of government is the prime minister, who is the leader of the political party with the most seats in the House. The head of state is the reigning British monarch, Queen Elizabeth II, as represented by the governor general, Sir Colville Young. The governor general is appointed by the party in power.

In the 2015 election, there were 196,587 eligible voters, or a little more than half of the population of Belize. The voting age is eighteen. The country has one of the highest voter-turnout rates in the world, and in the 2017 election approximately 73 percent of eligible voters made it out to the polls. Compare that to the United States, where only 55 percent of the population voted in 2016. In Canada it was 68.5 percent in the 2015 federal election.

• • • • •

The Belizean government works to make the country friendly to business; not so much billionaire-type businesses as small- and medium-sized enterprises. The kind of thing people can busy themselves with while they enjoy living in paradise.

Bob Hotchandani is a Belize success story. He came to the country from India in the mid-1960s. He started with nothing and today he owns everything from shops to real estate.

In Belize City, he and his son Sanjay have developed the Brown Sugar Market Place, named after an old sugar refinery on the water. It has the potential to become another cruise terminal. Bob Hotchandani is also a director of the Atlantic International Bank. This is a rags-to-riches story that, to my mind, shows what can be accomplished in a free and tolerant society like Belize.

Proof of just how easy it is to do business in Belize has been documented by the World Bank. It carries out an objective survey of just about every country, using complex measurements to determine what barriers there are to doing business. In a World Bank survey titled "Rankings on the Ease of Doing Business," Belize outstripped every country in the region.

To foster the development of entrepreneurship in the country, the Belize government has developed a program that allows business people to create what are

Rankings on the Ease of Doing Business 2008

(Lower numbers mean country is an easier place to do business)

Country	Rank
Belize	69
Panama	76
El Salvador	77
Nicaragua	96
Guatemala	116
Costa Rica	118
Honduras	134

called International Business Companies. Let's go further into that. An IBC is a company that is owned by a person who is not a resident of Belize and it conducts business with persons who are not residents of Belize. It does not conduct its business in Belize, but it can conduct its business from Belize and contact its client and customer base overseas by internet, telephone, services such as FedEx, and even the mail.

The IBC law is pretty much a carbon copy of a similar law in the British Virgin Islands. It was successful there with hundreds of thousands of IBCs set up to do business in the BVI.

Belize has caught up in a hurry. The country has around fifty thousand active International Business Companies with almost that many dormant companies registered. The government gets an annual fee of a minimum $150 from each of those companies, as well as the business income that is generated, in everything from legal fees and banking income to the money many of those people spend in Belize when they are here. An IBC requires only one shareholder and one director, and they can be the same person. Incorporating an IBC takes only twenty-four hours. Here are a few examples of the types of business you can conduct with an IBC:

- Hold intellectual property, such as copyrights and patents
- Hold real estate in another jurisdiction
- Investment holdings and asset protection
- Stock-trading account for trading on international markets
- Trade and ship goods from one country to another using an IBC. You pay no tax under Belize law,

though the "beneficial owner" might have to pay tax in his home jurisdiction.

Qualified Retired Person Program and Banking

Although Qualified Retired Persons have the benefits of near citizenship, they are classified as non-residents when it comes to banking. People who retire to Belize should open two bank accounts: a domestic account to handle day-to-day expenses in Belize currency and an international account to move money back and forth to their home jurisdiction. Also, you don't want to convert all your money to Belize dollars because there are costs involved in converting it back. Better to leave it in dollars, pounds, or Euros and convert into Belize dollars as needed. There are no charges for opening a domestic bank account and only minimal charges for transactions, similar to those in the United States and Canada.

• • • • •

Property taxes in Belize are generally pretty low compared to other regions, and lower still outside a town or a city. Moreover, taxes remain the same on land whether it has been developed or not. The intent of the legislation is, in fact, to make it easier to collect taxes. It means the government does not have to conduct evaluations; it just taxes at the same rate for everyone. In an undeveloped area, that amounts to about BZ$100 a year for an acre of property.

The interest rate on large foreign deposits in the fall of 2017 was 4 percent and the local head of the Atlantic

International Bank points out that there are no withholding taxes on that for foreign residents. So far the bank takes deposits in U.S. dollars and Euros. Atlantic says if foreign residents are looking for "heightened confidentiality," it advises going the IBC route. Still, there is no hiding cash because of new worldwide reporting rules imposed by the United States and other jurisdictions.

Clients can access their accounts from anywhere in the world via the internet. In the case of an IBC, however, the bank issues an electronic fob to the account holder, which generates a random password every thirty seconds to log in, giving the client a high level of security.

The bank also offers a credit card that can either be in the account holder's or the IBC's name. There is a catch: you have to maintain a balance at the bank of 125 percent of the card's credit limit. Still, it provides a way to anonymously spend your money and it earns interest at a Belizean bank. "We pay the card out at the end of the month, so there's never any interest to pay. So in effect it works like a debit card," says one banker from Belize.

• • • • •

Internet banking also allows third-party payments, so you can not only pay regular bills such as utilities, but also make payments to individuals and companies. It is like being able to write an electronic cheque.

• • • • •

The IT departments at banks in Belize have access to the best financial software in the world.

If you want to buy a property in Belize, local banks will lend you the money. Banks in the United States, Canada, or Europe are not going to give you a mortgage on a property in Belize, so the banks in Belize are the only option if you can't bring enough money from home. Also, if you want to go into business and develop a few properties of your own, the banks in Belize will work with you. Choose your bank carefully. Some are faster at loan approvals than others. Speak to a few expats and do some homework before you make any decisions.

"If you're doing any sort of real-estate transaction here we're the people to talk to. We know the market here. We give advice. Where to go, who is the right person to talk to," says one banker. He has some plain-spoken advice for newcomers: "We know who might try to scam you, so we give practical and money-saving advice to our clients."

CHAPTER 9

BANKING IN BELIZE

BEFORE discussing the banking system in Belize, I think it's important to make sure that newcomers to the country are aware that it has its own currency. People might ask why. Simply stated: having its own currency gives Belize independence to set interest rates and other monetary policies; countries such as Turks and Caicos that use United States currency are subject to interest rates and monetary policies set in Washington by the United States Federal Reserve Board, thereby losing fiscal autonomy.

By the way, there are official rules about the everyday use of currency in Belize. If a price in Belize is posted as dollars, then you have the right to pay for it in Belize dollars. Businesses can also post a price in U.S. dollars, but it must clearly say U.S. dollars. The same is true in contracts. On the other hand, mortgages given by international banks in Belize are never in Belize dollars; they are specified in U.S. or Canadian dollars, British pounds, or Euros.

Now to the banking system.

• • • • •

Bank of Nova Scotia in San Pedro.

The first bank in this country was the Bank of British Honduras, established over one hundred years ago. It was acquired by the Royal Bank of Canada and operated under that name with branches throughout the country. The big Canadian banks have a long history of operating in the region. Scotiabank — the Bank of Nova Scotia — opened its first branch in Belize in 1968 and now has eleven branches in the country.

Not only are large international banks continuing to open branches in Belize, new domestic banks continue to be opened. The advantage that Belize has to offer in starting a small bank is that it is cheap in terms of licence fees and annual capital requirements. For example, paid-up capital requirement for an unrestricted B class international banking licence is US$3 million. The last licence granted for an international bank was to a group from Canada who established the Choice Bank in mid-2007.

Belize Bank.

The five domestic banks cater to the local population, and the nine international banks deal with foreigners. The domestic banks operate only within the country and are subject to exchange-control regulations. Further, Belize banknotes are valid only in Belize and can't be exchanged outside the country. However, there is no control on foreign currency brought into the country, within the existing laws that cover money laundering.

One American dollar equals two Belize dollars. If you pay for something in a store with American money, you will almost always get your change back in Belize notes. From the biggest hotel to the smallest shopkeeper, everyone is fastidious about giving the right change for U.S. dollars.

Choice Bank

Choice Bank is a relatively new institution in Belize, and shows the type of opportunity available in the country. A group of investors from North America decided to take advantage of Belize's banking legislation and opened their own financial institution.

"There were a few reasons we chose Belize," says one of the founders. "It's English-speaking, a member of the British Commonwealth, and has some of the of the best trust laws in the world. People can set up their international business in Belize. As a bank that caters to non-Belizeans who are looking at international business, we don't really talk of it as offshore, but more international.

"Our focus as a bank is to service international businesses that are set up in Belize and for them to have the advantages of full-service banking, North American style. We are an international bank. We can do anything that any other bank can do in North America."

Much of Choice Bank's business is electronic, handling credit-card transactions for MasterCard. It is an example of the high-tech modern business that can run from Belize using the country's banking laws and the rules that created IBCs. Choice Bank's customers come from Mexico, Europe, South America, and North America.

Since it is an international bank, citizens of Belize cannot bank there. The bank is quick to point out that it does not deal in the type of banking secrecy that attracts international attention.

"That subject comes up all the time. Our bank is run by bankers and we follow all of the worldwide regulations on knowing your customer and preventing any money laundering. We do as much or more due diligence as a North American bank. So anybody who applies as a corporation or an individual to open a bank account with us, we do a world check on them. We don't take any money unless it comes in through wires from a recognized bank."

The international banks are not subject to controls and don't mix with the domestic banks. This explains why there is what my banker friends call a "ring fence" between hard-currency transactions and domestic-currency transactions. The rough definition of a hard currency is one from a developed country that has no currency restrictions. The U.S. and Canadian dollars, the British pound, and the Euro are the four hard currencies recognized by the banking system in Belize. In other words, foreigners can open an account with a foreign bank and conduct business in those four foreign currencies. Not all banks deal in all four currencies, but most do some combination.

Day-to-Day Banking

There are ATMs in all major centres. Service in domestic banks is improving, but it might not measure up to North American standards. Patience is a virtue: a cliché, but it is an attitude that wins a newcomer friends in Belize and saves a lot of unnecessary anxiety. Things will go slower in Belize so relax and learn to live with it. This is true not only with banking, but with a lot of other aspects of the country.

People operating international banks say they make a point of speeding up things such as credit applications so that foreign clients get the kind of service they are accustomed to. Banks are aiming to approve loans within a week of receiving the applications.

One of the secrets to efficient personal banking is to never go into a branch. I remember reading an article by the late Malcolm Forbes saying one of the reasons he could do all the things he did was he cut out time-wasting activity. One of those was standing in line at banks. Of course, back then his secretary did it. Today we are used to internet banking and electronic transfers. That ease of use is here in many ways in Belize, and it is getting more efficient all the time.

Mortgages and Loans

Recently, international banks in Belize have become extremely active on the mortgage front. "Belize is still seen as a very hot destination for investing in real estate," says Ricardo Pelayo of Atlantic International Bank. "Mortgages are one of the primary components of our business model. We provide mortgages to purchase a lot or a property as a second home or for retirement purposes on loans anywhere from $100,000 to up somewhere around $2.2 million."

On the lending side, the majority of the foreign customers at Belize banks are Americans, followed by Canadians. Banks in Belize are keen to lend money to foreigners to buy property or finance businesses. As a foreigner, you can borrow from a domestic or an international bank; however, the domestic banks have significantly higher interest rates, so you'd be well advised to borrow from an international bank, if you qualify.

If you need money to buy property in Belize, you might think of borrowing against assets in your home country. For example, interest rates are much lower in the United States or Canada so you could borrow against your property or business there, and then bring the money to Belize.

On the flip side, deposit rates are much higher in Belize. Interest on a $1 million deposit is 4 percent or higher (as of late 2017). That is more than double the return on a U.S. or Canadian ten-year bond.

Secrecy Laws

Belize's banking system has changed dramatically since we published the first edition of this book. Banking in Belize has a lot to offer the expat or retired person moving to Belize, but not banking secrecy. That is a thing of the past, because of new regulations imposed by the United States and other major economies. Instead, there is transparency. Any transfer or other banking activity has to be reported to the American or other authorities.

Banking secrecy used to be thought of as numbered accounts in Switzerland, cash hidden from the outside world. Belize was, for a time, the Switzerland of Central America. No more.

Ricardo Pelayo, CEO of the Atlantic International Bank, says his institution still offers the same services as it always has, with one major exception: Belize banks are no longer below the radar.

"What has changed significantly is the way business is done, because of regulatory issues that have come along, such as FATCA, which is the Foreign Contact Compliance Act for the United States. You now have GCCA, which is for the rest of the world," says Mr. Pelayo.

"Those days of trying to hide assets and avoid taxes are gone. Atlantic International never targeted that kind of client. We've always targeted those who want to invest in this country," says Mr. Pelayo. "I think there is still room to manage taxes. There are structures that can facilitate the movement of property to heirs with minimum taxation."

Christopher Coye is an American-trained economist who once worked for the Central Bank of Belize, and is also a lawyer who has practiced in the country for eighteen years. He agrees that the days of Belize being thought of as an offshore tax haven are over.

"There has been an immense change in banking in Belize, and pressure from the Americans has significantly affected the way the banks do business in Belize," he says. Coye worked for a large international bank until 2013, and is now involved in law and real-estate development on Ambergris Caye. If Belize has an establishment, he is at the pinnacle, politically, legally, and from a business perspective. He says the new banking laws in the U.S. and elsewhere imposed a hardship on the banking industry.

The rules meant that for a short period banks in Belize were not able to deal with other big international banks, the system known as correspondent banking.

"For a couple of years, the offshore banks lost their corresponding relationships. They call it de-risking. The banks in Belize are too small to comply with the risk associated with these banks. Offshore banks took most of the hit but the domestic banks also lost a corresponding banking relationship so it was really a scary moment for our banking system and our economy," says Mr. Coye.

Atlantic International Bank and others have regained their correspondent banking status.

"There was a period where several banks, including ourselves, had lost correspondent banking relationships that we depend on to move money anywhere in the world. But in the case of Atlantic International, we were able to get back correspondent banking within a month so there was only that short period of a month where we were without it. We work with two banks: one out of Puerto Rico and the other one out of London," says Mr. Pelayo.

The banking laws in Belize do not cover noncriminal tax matters and things such as alimony.

"Our banking is international banking. We can conduct business with businesses in Belize. We can conduct business with residents of Belize, provided that those residents are operating a business in the special free trade zones near the border. For the most part it's hard currency, foreign exchange business that you can conduct in Belize."

Banking and International Business Companies

As mentioned earlier, IBCs allow foreign residents to incorporate in Belize. The owners or directors of the firm do not have to be residents or citizens of Belize and there is no requirement to have a domestic office or to hire local people.

There are no taxes or foreign exchange controls on IBCs, which can be used to carry on financial transactions, even for something as basic as a securities trading account. It can also be used to own business assets outside Belize. The restrictions that do exist stipulate that IBCs can't do business in Belize or with the country's citizens or residents. That restriction applies to owning real estate in Belize or domestic financial transactions in banking or insurance.

The ownership structure is simple. An International Business Company requires only one shareholder and one director, which can be the same person or corporation. Incorporating an IBC can cost as little as $700 plus a $150 annual fee, depending on the capitalization of the firm. That compares to initial costs of $15,000 or more in other jurisdictions.

IBC Fees

The Government of Belize charges the following annual renewal fee (in USD) for an IBC:

- IBC with share capital of $50,000: $150
- IBC with share capital over $50,000: $1,000
- IBC with no par value: $350

International Business Companies Registry of Belize
Marina Towers, Suite 201
Newtown Barracks
Belize City, Belize
Central America
Telephone Number: +501-223-5108
Fax Number: +501-223-5124
Email: info@ibcbelize.com
Website: www.ibcbelize.com

Trusts

Trusts set up in Belize provide an excellent way to protect assets. The Trusts Act of 1992 was another far-sighted financial reform that has helped make modern Belize more attractive to foreign investors. The legislation allows people from outside the country to set up trusts whose beneficiaries can be a person, a charity, or a combination of the two.

There are discretionary and purpose trusts. The discretionary trust is by far the most popular. It protects the person setting it up, the beneficiary of the trust, and the assets within it. Under local laws of financial

The colonial architecture of Belize City in what was once British Honduras.

Aerial view of Manta Resort at Glover's Atoll.

confidentiality, the contents of the trust are secret once it is registered with Belize's Supreme Court. Once that is done, only the trustee can authorize releasing details of the trust. This has already been tested in 1994 when the Supreme Court of Belize refused a request from the United States Securities and Exchange Commission, which was seeking information in a case it was pursuing.

The law in Belize states that as long as there was no fraud involved in establishing the trust, no foreign authority can go after its assets. That includes assets in a marriage breakup, a contested will outside Belize, or assets involved in a bankruptcy in another country. The key point in the setting up of the trust is that no fraud was committed in Belize itself.

The best advice is to contact local lawyers who specialize in trusts. See Appendix A for contact information.

Banking for Retirees

People who retire to Belize can also take advantage of banking in Belize and ownership of an IBC. Most banks can handle all the paperwork.

"When people qualify under the retirement program, they automatically maintain their non-resident status even though they are physically living here in Belize," says a senior local banker. "That means they can bank with an international bank, they can have an IBC, and can do things that I can't do as a citizen of Belize."

The Qualified Retired Person is also allowed to shop in the duty-free zones located near the borders with Mexico and Guatemala, something Belizeans can't do. Many things are cheaper in these zones, including gasoline and diesel fuel. Then there are people who aren't ready to retire. They can also use the banking and legal system in Belize.

Let's take the example of a consultant. He can do his work anywhere in the world. And contract it out to the IBC. You leave that money in Belize and unless you pay yourself back in Canada, for example, there is no tax. The IBC itself could then have a credit card that you can use anywhere in the world, but the account is paid by the IBC from your bank account in Belize. It doesn't take much imagination to recognize the advantages of this system.

Technology makes Belize even more attractive than when I first wrote about this. Perhaps the biggest thing is the internet speed. You see business people sitting at breakfast on the beach at Ramon's in Ambergris Caye. They could be doing online banking, checking on accounts located thousands of miles away or right down the street. Inexpensive phone and data plans that didn't even exist a few years ago mean keeping in touch on your home number is fast and cheap.

Belize is that wonderful mix of the modern and the remote. A connected piece of paradise. The owner of an IBC is now more independent, whether working in Belize or outside the country. People who retire to Belize, or spend a long stretch of the winter there, are now connected to the outside world as never before. The good news is that the internet technology in Belize is only going to become faster and cheaper under current government plans.

CHAPTER 10
REAL ESTATE

TIMING is everything in real estate.

People always repeat the mantra of "location, location, and location." But there is no point showing up at a location once it's hot. You've missed the action. If you want to invest or develop a property in Barbados, St. Barts, or Costa Rica, you're too late.

Say you bought some land or a house in Costa Rica in the past few years. There is little doubt you bought in at the top, or what we'll look back on and see as the top sometime in the next decade when the smoke has cleared. You won't have to say that about buying in Belize now, because, in my experience, when a place has this much value it cannot become the easy victim of phenomena like the recent recessions.

In every major downturn there are always stories of people who were smart enough to get in at the bottom, at the right time and the right place.

Belize now is one of those places.

When I first went in search of a place to invest and develop in the warmer parts of the western hemisphere, I used the same principles and techniques as I did back home in Canada. The basic numbers are simple. There are eighty million people who will be retiring in North

America over the next two decades and 90 percent of them are Americans. Those numbers shoot even higher when you include Europe, Japan, and Asian countries that have a prosperous business and middle class, such as India, South Korea, and China. There are also people from Eastern Europe and Russia who are now rich by Western standards.

Many of these people want second homes. For those who are adventurous and want to go outside the crowded retirement areas in the United States, Belize is just a two-hour flight from major cities such as Atlanta, Houston, and Miami, and a four- to five-hour flight from New York City and Toronto.

As a contrarian I know that the time to buy is when other people are selling. When the headlines scream about subprime mortgages, foreclosures, and the decline in the value of real estate, it is the time to be on the lookout for a bargain. The people of the English-speaking countries of the world utilize property as a way to build wealth. In the United States, Canada, Britain, and Australia, more than 60 percent of the population own their own homes. No doubt a lot of people overdid it in the last real-estate boom, but bubbles are like that; and history has taught us that bubbles create opportunities.

My real-estate philosophy is this: on the macro level, be counter-cyclical. When everybody's selling you should be buying, doing the opposite of what the market is doing. On a micro level, watch for inefficiencies in the market.

This philosophy is based on numbers. It isn't the kind of complex formula that the mathematicians invented for the derivative and credit-swap markets. My ideas are simple. Some may be familiar, but I am restating them as they are related to my real-estate business, in Canada and, in particular, in Belize:

Investing in Real Estate by the Numbers

1. Supply: Ambergris Caye has a limited supply of land, like Vancouver in my Canadian operations, or like Manhattan, an extreme example in the United States. These are places, like Singapore, Dubai, and Hong Kong, where real estate appreciates because of shortages of land.
2. Demand: The *Wall Street Journal* estimates eleven thousand people *a day* retire in the United States. That's eighty million people over the next twenty years and a lot of them are looking for a second place to live: Belize is it. Warm weather, close to home, and just a couple hours' direct flight from major airports such as Miami and Houston. All you need is 1 percent of that eighty million to create a boom.
3. Half a million: That is how many Canadians spend their winters in Florida and Arizona. If just fifty thousand of them decided to spend their winters in Belize — where the tax and banking regimes are more attractive — there would be a boom in a country of 358,823.
4. Belize prices in Euros: When you look at what Belize costs for Europeans, there will almost certainly be more of them coming as tourists and retirees. It is already happening. There is an Air France pilot living on Caye Caulker and an Italian couple running a restaurant there.
5. Think of these numbers: Europeans have annual vacations of five weeks or more and they are used to paying £400 for a hotel room. What will happen when more of them discover tropical sea and sun at 1960s prices? Belize, with its rainforests, islands, uncrowded

beaches, Mayan ruins, and diving, has more to offer than a crowded, overpriced Caribbean island.

6. I told you so: In this space in 2011 I mused, "The ubiquitous Boeing 737 can make it from Canada to Belize without refuelling." Now WestJet is flying the 737 in four hours from Toronto and Air Canada is doing the same with an Airbus. Since last fall WestJet has been flying from Calgary to Belize City once a week. Belize is on the ground floor in the development stakes, where Costa Rica and Barbados were twenty-five years ago.
7. Borrowing to buy: Credit is available in Belize. The country's international banking system makes it easy for foreign residents to finance the purchase of property.
8. Land survey system runs on the British model: The top surveyors in Belize are trained in Britain in the Chartered Surveyors tradition.

Lazy days in the sun at Costa del Sol.

What to Buy

Perhaps the easiest route is to buy an existing condo. It's perfect for someone who wants an extended-stay holiday home, especially in one of the resorts being developed.

Belize offers a lot of different properties to suit different lifestyles. Want a back-to-nature getaway? There are simple wooden structures on remote islands or deep in the rainforest. But most people are looking for something a little more familiar. Whether it's a condo or a house, it is available in Belize.

Someone wanting to mimic the life they're used to back home can buy or construct a modern concrete house built to take advantage of all the beauty of Belize. Not only can it be on a beachfront — an increasingly rare commodity in the modern world — it can be made with local touches such as doors and cabinetry built from mahogany or other native hardwoods.

Luxury beach huts on Blackbird Caye.

Buying a lot and building your own house can be the best way of doing things. You pick the location to suit your lifestyle: there's a big difference between living near the beach, on an isolated caye, or on the edge of the rainforest. Lot prices are highest in and around San Pedro. A lot in Costa del Sol sold for US$760,000 in mid-2017. It is a large lot, on the water, and beside some new multi-million-dollar houses.

A hundred feet of beachfront, raw land, in the village of San Pedro will fetch $1,000,000. It is perhaps the hottest spot in Belize. Prices drop off dramatically in areas outside Ambergris Caye. You can find property in the main village of Caye Caulker for $300,000.

Remember, when you get away from waterfront properties, prices can fall off a cliff.

Building your own house means you get the design you want and you can monitor the quality of the construction. Construction costs in Belize are much lower than they are in the United States and Canada. Europeans would be shocked at how much cheaper it is to build here than in Britain or France.

"Building costs run around US$125 a square foot for wood and US$150 for concrete and that usually includes things such as septic cisterns. If you spend a little more you get real upscale construction," says a Belize property specialist. "This is on the island of Ambergris Caye. If you build on the mainland it will be cheaper."

Labour is the same across Belize and its islands: a good, qualified tradesman gets US$50 a day; a labourer, US$25 a day. Dirt cheap by world standards, but the reality is per capita income is $8,200 in Belize, compared to $57,300 in the United States and $46,300 in Canada (Source: CIA *World Factbook*, 2017, all figures in U.S. dollars). As an aside, Belize has the third-highest per capita income in Central America.

The reality of building in Belize is that things are usually slower than they would be in the United States or Canada. If you decide to save money and work as your own contractor, you can expect delays. Work with a reputable local contractor and things will move along faster.

Brad Campbell owns two luxury villas on Costa del Sol and bought eight more lots in 2017. In all, he and his father, Gar Campbell, own ten acres on Costa del Sol.

"It's a perfect location. Just five minutes by boat across the lagoon from San Pedro and it's quiet and remote," says Brad, who is a semi-retired businessman from Langley, British Columbia. "My main focus now is Belize."

In addition to his villas, he has built a separate property to house his caretaker and his family. They live on the second floor; downstairs is a garage and water treatment facility. He has also built a seawall and a two-hundred-foot pier.

They own a quarter-acre lot on the water on the San Pedro side to use as a staging area for guests. It is a short walk from the airport and the guests are then whisked across the lagoon to Costa del Sol.

The Campbells rent their properties out through CasasdelaCayevillas.com.

Those not wanting to build could buy something that has just been finished.

My friend Gabriel Kirchberger just bought Brahma Blue on Costa del Sol. He is upgrading it, and by the time he finishes, it will be the kind of first-class accommodation with extras you would expect in upmarket getaways such as St. Barts or the south coast of Barbados.

Gabriel also owns beautiful properties on Costa del Sol, each of which comes with fabulous features such as an infinity pool. In the high season, a three-bedroom villa rents for US$3,000 a week. A six-bedroom unit is US$5,000 to US$7,000 a week, Gabriel usually stays in his Costa del Sol properties throughout the year, but in April last year he had to stay at Ramon's in San Pedro because all of his units were rented.

There is an island called Hermit Caye for sale, an isolated 7.5-acre getaway in the Stann Creek area, on the market for just under $3 million. This sort of thing is not available anywhere else in the world. Another island sold for about that price in the spring of 2010.

Then there's the dream of living in a wooden shack in the wilderness on an isolated piece of land. Such places are available, but be careful what you wish for. Properties can be too basic — the Belize version of the log cabin — and too isolated. One man wanted to sell his wooden cottage and listed it on the internet. The interest was such that he got 4,600 hits. He narrowed it down to just two buyers, but both of them walked away. The cottage, while in good shape, was too rustic for them. The other drawback was its location, more than ten miles from San Pedro, so getting to town meant either hiring a water taxi or owning a boat. It was cheap enough, though; he was asking $219,000 — an example of the kind of escape you can find in Belize.

In the next section, let's take a look at what you can buy in three price ranges, all in U.S. dollars.

Where to Buy

Deciding where to buy property in Belize depends on who you are and what you want out of life. If you're heading to Belize for retirement, your needs are different than those of someone who is looking to develop a resort or a condo. A real-estate developer will be building condos, houses, or land-banking for future development. I specialize in a combination of all three.

Belize is the ideal place for the experienced real-estate developer who isn't ready to fully retire, but who wants to have a project with which to keep busy. The retirement rules combined with the business and banking laws make this easy to do in Belize.

Then there's the question of just how much you're willing to spend. But remember, whatever you buy will deliver capital appreciation over the long haul. Belize presents value for money at every level and in every location. There are four or five hot spots in Belize: Ambergris Caye, Caye Caulker, Placencia, Cayo, and Hopkins. Placencia is on the southern coast of the country fronting on the Caribbean. It has a quiet lifestyle and few of the restaurants or the nightlife of San Pedro.

"There's a big difference between San Pedro and Placencia," says a developer friend of mine. "For one thing San Pedro has been there a lot longer. We're also going to see a real marina going in there. Between Cancún and Cozumel, you don't have a real marina until you get down to Rio Dulce in Guatemala."

The marina will make it easier for large ships — though not cruise ships — to dock at Placencia. There are already new developments in Placencia that are along the lines of the gated communities that are so popular

There's still plenty of room in affordable Belize.

Real estate for sale.

in southern Florida. Placencia will soon have an international airport, and that will create demand for property, with direct flights from the United States and possibly Canada. When you think about it, it's quite something for a small country such as Belize to have two airlines and two international airports. There could well be a third at the north end of Ambergris Caye.

Hopkins is a Garifuna village in Stann Creek District. Sitting on the Caribbean Sea, it is framed to the west by the Maya Mountains. From Hopkins you can see Victoria Peak, which at 3,688 feet is the second highest mountain in Belize. The tallest, nearby Doyle's Delight, is just twelve feet higher. There are already half a dozen resorts here, and more are being developed.

Another up-and-coming location is Corozal near the Mexican border. One investor has close to a thousand acres of land there that he is going to develop as a total destination resort completed with golf course. At the moment, there are only two golf courses in Belize.

Caye Caulker, long a hideaway for some of the more unconventional tourists, is an ideal spot to get away from it all. Dangriga is another secondary beachfront location. All these places may be below the radar, but they have a fantastic view of the ocean. Someone in their forties might say, "I am going to retire in ten or fifteen years and by that time these places will be hot."

It can't be stated often enough that, as with other investments, there's always a ceiling on valuation, though there is never a ceiling in valuation on a beachfront property.

For people who have energy and imagination, there are many opportunities. The district of Orange Walk, for example, is an ideal place for organic farming. The land is cheap, and there is a twelve-month growing season and plenty of water for irrigation. Local labour is available at wage rates unheard of in the United States. A lot of the land hasn't been used for farming since the time of the Maya, so it is not worn out. Belize is perfect for this type of venture because of its proximity to the United States, where there is such a demand for organic products. The country's microclimates are ideal for other specialized agriculture, such as vineyards, specialty fruits, and tea gardens.

The Cayo District couldn't be more different than the coastal part of Belize. Government statistics show there are more Canadian expats in Cayo than anywhere else in Belize. It is the largest district in Belize and more than 60 percent of it is devoted to natural parks and reserves. It is a mixture involving mountains — including the Maya mountain range — as well as Mayan temples. A good starting point to any tour of this area would be San Ignacio. If you're mildly adventurous, try cave tubing, a sport unique to Belize. There is a lot of farming in the hill country there and if you're looking for a unique place to live away from the rest of the world, this is it.

How to Buy

Take your time. Don't rush down to Belize and fall in love with the first place you see and then ignore the rest of the country. After you've picked the location where you want to buy, you should find a reputable real-estate agent, hire a good lawyer, and make sure the property survey is done properly.

Here are my seven steps on how to buy property in Belize:

1. Visit Belize at least twice and go to islands such as Ambergris Caye and Caye Caulker, then to towns such as Hopkins, Placencia, and Cayo.

2. Use a reputable local real-estate agency, preferably one with a franchise. These international firms have a code of ethics.
3. At home in Canada and the United States we sometimes buy condos at pre-construction prices. You could be waiting for a long time if you make an emotional buy. Sometimes you're better off to buy a finished product, unless you're dealing with a big reputable developer.
4. Negotiate hard. There are always two prices, one for emotional tourists and another for serious investors. There are always the people who get off the plane, fall desperately in love with Belize, and write a cheque. Study the market and negotiate hard.
5. Do you need financing? International banks in Belize are a special category and they specialize in providing financing to foreign buyers. The rates are a little bit higher than in North America. (See Appendix A for a list of all the banks.) Financing can take sixty to ninety days to secure. Be patient.
6. Get a seasoned real-estate lawyer from Belize to do a title search. Don't use anyone but a lawyer. The process is much easier than in Mexico or Costa Rica. There are no foreign ownership restrictions and no capital gains tax. Belize has been reforming its land system since 1980, making a gradual transition to the Registered Land Act System. It is simpler and easier to deal with than the old Torrens system. More than half the country has switched to the new system. Check which one covers the property you're interested in.
7. Be careful. Some people make the mistake of buying a property, whether it is a house, condo, or lot, with a

promise of title in the future. Use local professionals to make sure you're protected.

8. Title insurance is available.

Belize has a "stamp tax," which is, in effect, a land-transfer tax equal to 5 percent of the final price of the house. It is paid by the buyer. There is a slight wrinkle: "Stamp duty with regard to land transfer is 5 percent of the purchase price less US$10,000. For example, if you purchase a property for US$100,000, you will only pay 5 percent on US$90,000," says Shiromi Thuraiaiyah, manager at Atlantic International Bank.

Along with the legal and search fees, that should bring the total closing costs to 6 or 7 percent. The property prices in Belize are substantially lower than in Turks and Caicos and the Bahamas. But they are higher than in some less-developed Central American counties such as Nicaragua.

The Advantages of the Survey System in Belize

- detailed title deed
- separate Ministry of Lands in Belize
- lot size and plan exact
- modelled on British and Canadian system
- Belize surveyors train in Canada and Britain
- Americans are at home with survey details
- land commission – makes registering land easier
- title insurance is available

The rules for land ownership and surveying are all but identical to those in most English-speaking countries. Belize is gradually changing its system of measuring and registering land so that it is in accord with those rules. Land registry in Belize used to work under the Torrens system, but that was reformed with the Registered Land Act of 1980. Now the Registered Land Act System is not based on maps and surveys; rather, it is based on getting a simple piece of paper: a land certificate with a map attached.

Most of Belize has been reorganized under this simplified registration system, and that makes it even easier to identify lots and acreage. The land at Costa del Sol, a few minutes across the water from San Pedro, is one part of the country that falls under the new land registration system. All condominiums are under the new surveying system.

A beachfront villa on Costa de Sol.

"It is so simple you don't need a lawyer except to check the root of title and to make sure someone else hasn't bought it before and this sort of thing," said a prominent lawyer in Belize City. "The system is very modern and very reliable. People still go out and do measurements of the property."

The Platinum Coast

"Platinum Coast" was what I exclaimed out loud when I first saw this shimmering location. It is a long stretch of sandy coves and beaches facing the open sea. The Platinum Coast is a little less than a mile in from the tip of our property. There are fourteen miles of natural white sand beaches and thirty-six bays that jut in and out of the coastline, each providing privacy and isolation from the bay just around the corner. The development started as a stretch of untouched land with views across the calm blue sea.

The property faces west, away from the surf toward Dolphin Bay, across the water from Leonardo DiCaprio's resort on 104-acre Blackadore Caye, which he bought for US$1.75 million. It is expected to open in 2018.

Here is a snippet from the *New York Times* on DiCaprio's development: "A well-known environmental activist, Mr. DiCaprio bought Blackadore Caye, 104 acres of wild, unpopulated land off the coast of Belize, with a partner soon after he set foot in the country a decade ago. 'It was like heaven on earth,' he said, speaking by telephone from Los Angeles. 'And almost immediately, I found this opportunity to purchase an island there.'"

From the Platinum Coast that island appears as a glimmering green diamond in the azure sea. It is the only spot that gets the sunrise and sunset on the water.

This is also the place that inspired my phrase "the last virgin paradise." Until now, humans never had a reason to venture to this narrow strip of sand and earth covered with light green vegetation. It isn't arable, but it is peaceful. The bays and inlets face the sunset with only a few islands dotting the horizon. We own the closest island and are preserving it as a bird and wildlife sanctuary. The buildings here, however, will be so unobtrusive that much of the wildlife will stay. The property is far enough off the coast of mainland Belize that even though it faces west you can't see the land from here. Because it's the most stunning strip of property, I wanted to save the development here until the last. That is why there is nothing there now, though there soon will be. We're going to try to keep everything as natural as possible and build around the beauty of the place.

Where developers are building, we ensure they manicure the bushes and try to keep everything looking pretty much the way it did when I first came here. Of course, you have to move things to build, but we're going to disturb nature as little as possible. This is truly an environmentally friendly development.

What I want to see built on our 2,700-acre property — and we control what goes up on the Platinum Coast — are high-end luxury houses, low-rise condos, and 100-percent-green resorts. There already are some low-rise condos, a spa, and some single-family houses. Brahma Blue is a four-storey luxury building that is being refreshed and repurposed by Canadian businessman Gabriel Kirchberger, who already owns other properties on Costa del Sol.

There is another development planned just off the south end of my property. My raw land surrounds this development, which is in the advanced planning stage. This is a case of wait, and the world comes to you.

North Ambergris Caye

One of the areas that has really taken off since I wrote the first edition of this book is the north end of Ambergris Caye. For openers, there is a paved road that goes quite a way north once you cross the short bridge out of San Pedro. There are condo developments, some of them beautiful pink buildings in front of natural beaches, small boutique hotels, and the new Wyndham Grand, which is profiled in Chapter 4.

"The north side has really picked up with luxury properties and I think that with the addition of this flag and other flags to come in the future, it really puts Belize on the radar and I think that goes to promote a very robust tourism sector," says Jeremy Meighan, owner and partner of the Wyndham, which is set to open in 2018.

The municipal government has made a conscious decision to expand to the north. The mayor of Ambergris Caye may have his office in San Pedro, but he is charge of the whole island.

"Most of the development is happening on the north, which is the bigger and the wider area," says Danny Guerrero. He also plans to improve access to the north by widening the bridge from San Pedro.

Some friends of mine from Los Angeles were here in 2017 and toured the entire area looking for an investment property. They finally settled on a ten-acre lot at the far north end of Ambergris Caye. I think they were pretty prescient.

It is not all high-end. There is a place called Secret Beach that is beyond where the new paved road ends. You can get there by car, but if you take a golf cart the road can be little rough. The best way is to go in by boat. Secret Beach is not as secret as it used to be. The place is packed with young people. There is a bar and restaurant, some rental cottages, and of course a beach. A great way to spend a few hours on a sunny afternoon.

"The south is developing a little slower," says Mayor Guerrero. "But there is a huge development on the extreme south of the island, the La Sirene, with big celebrity basketball stars purchasing on that project. We actually have Kareem Abdul-Jabbar involved there, along with other basketball players. That project has sold over 45 percent."

From the south end of Ambergris Caye to the north there is fresh development: high-end luxury in the south, luxury and boutique hotels just over the bridge at the end of San Pedro, and good old-fashioned raw opportunity in the north. Plenty of room to get in at either end.

New Construction in Belize

The world wants to go green and Belize is no exception. The government and businesses in Belize know that going green is the smart thing to do. The town of San Pedro was green out of necessity, collecting rainwater, treating sewage, and encouraging the use of solar panels before green became the rage.

I don't build things in Belize, but I do set standards for what is built at Costa del Sol. There are low-level condos sitting on the waterfront with spaces and features that are the equal of those in any major world resort. New beach houses are already up and more are planned for the large lots along the shoreline. One of my favourites is a spectacular residence on Costa del Sol built by a close friend of mine in Belize. I'll use it as an example of the quality of new construction you can see in Belize. The roof is the first thing you might notice. Rather than rising to a peak, it curves and folds into itself from both sides. This is more than a pretty design; it has serious functions that fit in with the green, sustainable plan for the area. First, the roof funnels the winds blowing off the coast into the house, creating a permanent breeze: nature's air conditioning. No need for all-day energy-wasting air conditioners. Second, it collects rainwater, which runs into a cistern that is in fact the foundation for the entire house. This huge reservoir holds fifty thousand gallons of fresh water used for showers, the dishwasher, the clothes washer, the swimming pool, irrigation, and everything except drinking water. The underground reservoir keeps the water fresh and cool.

Solar panels, which you can barely see from the outside because of the way the roof folds in, heat water and supplement the electricity supply from the national power grid.

The home's interior is unique. Building a home like this in Belize is like buying a tailor-made suit. The builder avoided using any prefab pieces; even the door frames are custom-made to fit the rooms with their tall ceilings. To give it a warm feeling, the indigenous hardwoods of Belize are used to dramatic effect. Dark mahogany and lighter rosewood combine to make the multihued dark shutters for the windows. Custom-made doors of

The author at Costa del Sol, a five-minute boat ride from San Pedro.

exotic local wood give the interior a striking appearance. It sounds expensive, but this is one of the advantages of building a new home in Belize; local woods are cheap compared to those in North America or Europe, and so are local carpenters and cabinet makers who know how to work with the native trees.

Gabriel Kirchberger owns several properties on Costa del Sol and he uses local Mennonites for construction and fine carpentry.

"Mennonites are superb for woodwork, furniture, and painting. They are also excellent roofers and can do landscaping," says Mr. Kirchberger, a native of Germany who speaks German to the Mennonites. "They have an unbelievable work ethic."

Tropical woods are one of the things that make any new house in Belize unique. The cost of using these exotic woods would be prohibitive in any other beachfront resort in the world. Along with mahogany, they include teak, rosewood, and a number of other trees, many of which are known by their Spanish or Mayan names. If you're worried about the rainforest being mown down to produce these precious woods, you can rest easy. One of the new sustainable farming businesses in Belize is planting valuable trees for future harvest.

I own a 1,500-acre rainforest in Belize, most of it mahogany. It will *never* be clear-cut. When there is a harvest each tree will be carefully selected and cut so as not to damage any others. It takes twenty-five years to grow a mahogany tree to maturity, a little less for teak. The other hardwoods are now managed in this sustainable way, so you don't have to worry about using them in building projects. Wild trees are preserved in national parks and sanctuaries.

• • • • •

While hurricanes are rare in Belize, they are a reality, so new buildings and infrastructure are built to take the worst. For example, the electrical junction boxes in our development are raised four feet off the ground, in case of a tidal surge. A four-foot rise is about the worst that could hit the San Pedro area. New properties are built to take the wind and the water. Under the light covering of earth and sand is solid bedrock. At the start of construction, builders break up the bedrock and then mix it with concrete and anchor the foundation to the bedrock. In most cases, the thick cement walls are made from poured concrete rather than concrete block and that gives them more structural strength. In my friend's new house, even the stairs are concrete, attached by rebar to the outside walls.

The builder jokingly describes it as a bomb shelter. The lower windows are another design feature; they open to allow stormwater and wind to pass through the house. The furniture and other household effects would be safe upstairs and a storm would do almost no damage to the concrete structure below. This is an extreme example; as I mention elsewhere, hurricanes are rare, but it's better to be prepared.

Waste water could be a problem, but here too there is an elegant solution. With the bedrock close to the surface there is nowhere for water to disperse as it would in a normal septic-tank system. Instead, new construction uses special septic tanks that have an aerobic system to break down the sewage. That water, 99 percent clean, is used to irrigate plants. There are other creative uses for water. When it comes to rain, it's feast or famine in coastal Belize. There can be long periods of dry, sunny weather. Good for people spending a lot of time here, not so great for the greenery and other plant life. That's why new construction on Costa del Sol uses grey water — generated by washing dishes, showering, and so on — to water plants. It is discreetly channelled to feed the roots of everything from palm trees to flower beds. And, of course, during periods of drought is when things such as the fifty-thousand-gallon reservoir under the house come into play.

These design elements are being used in all of the modern buildings on Costa del Sol. Not only does it make a lot of economic sense, it also gives the owner eco-bragging rights, to be able to say how much he's doing for the environment, while saving energy and money at the same time.

Green and Affordable Belize

Belize is one of the last places in the world where middle-class North Americans can afford to buy beachfront property. Going green has a lot of appeal. There is the feel-good factor: people like to think they're doing something about the environment. When your children try to guilt you for not being green enough, you can point out that your carbon use is minute, if you are living in one of the new developments in Belize like the one I'm working on.

It also makes economic sense. In my apartment buildings in Canada, I use the most sustainable techniques to keep my operating costs low. In Belize we're doing the same thing, but we've taken it to a whole new level. It does not require an austere lifestyle: you can still have high-speed internet at the same time as you have no cars.

One example of this is a local businessman who has a three-bedroom fishing camp on isolated Blackbird Caye. He has solar panels on the roof and a couple of small wind turbines ($4,000 each) all feeding into a bank of twelve high-tech batteries. He uses the power to run all the lights, a couple of fans, and the radio, and to recharge his laptop computer. There are three satellites on the roof: one for TV, another for an internet connection, and a third for SiriusXM satellite radio. If he needs more power, he is hooked into Blackbird Caye's electrical power system. "I do it to be independent and to be ecologically correct. It's a pain bringing out the diesel and also dangerous if you have a spill," he says.

Solar power used to be the stuff of dreams, but *The Economist* recently pointed out that it is cheaper to generate electricity from solar than from coal, and the price of solar panels keeps falling. Going green isn't some fashionable slogan, but just plain economic sense. Supplying solar energy presents a tremendous business opportunity in sunny Belize.

"The potential is huge. You could run the entire island of San Pedro, as well as Belize, from renewable energy sources. Solar is a better solution but wind is also a possibility for the simple reason that if you integrate both of them it actually makes more sense," says Jaspal Deol, a registered electrical engineer from California who is doing solar and renewable consulting in Belize, in particular on my island.

One of the things about Costa del Sol is that it caters to a wide group of people: low-rise condos accommodate those who prefer intimate luxury; beachfront houses appeal to those who want the prestige of a larger property; down the road, exclusive resorts will offer a taste of life in paradise for those who don't want to make a total commitment to living here.

Look at the price of real estate in the Caribbean from St. Kitts and Nevis to Barbados. All but 1 percent of the world is priced out of those markets. And I'm speaking here of the millionaire-next-door types, people who have saved and are comfortable — and are looking for a beachfront getaway — but aren't in the category of the superrich. They just can't afford the Caribbean, period. You just have to be a lot richer than even the upper end of retiring baby boomers to live anywhere in the Caribbean, even Jamaica. This is not true for Belize. It's affordable, sustainable, and livable in a relaxed, yet luxurious way.

CHAPTER 11
TOURISM

THERE'S a certain sameness to many Caribbean resorts that gets up my nose. Sure they're warm and the sight of the heaving sea still thrills me, but the resorts and the restaurants have a uniform — almost studied — quaintness that I don't like.

Development and tourism in Belize are more boutique than mass-market. The word *boutique* does not mean it is just for the rich. This has nothing to do with price. Belize is already attractive for backpackers who want a unique experience and for middle-class families who don't want to be shoved into a boring high-rise hotel. Cancún is mass-market; Belize is boutique. Both tourism and development are at the ground-floor stage now, and the country is attracting smaller and more upscale resorts rather than Mexico's banks of high-rise hotels and the similar mass-market tourism of southern Florida.

Not Belize. It is a Club Med–free zone and a country that is, to my way of thinking, a one-off. It's what Belize doesn't have that makes it stand apart from mainstream resorts. It doesn't have one Club Med, Starbucks, or McDonald's; and no planeloads of tourists descending from low-cost charter flights. The charter-flight

Annual Tourist Arrivals in Central America (2016)		
Country	**Area**	**Tourists**
Belize	386,000	1,005,000
Costa Rica	2,925,000	N.A.
El Salvador	1,434,000	618,000
Guatemala	1,585,000	332,000
Honduras	908,000	1,359,000

Source: Central American Tourist Organization.

Who Visits Belize Now? (2015)		
Region	**No. of Tourists**	**Overall Percentage**
United States	215,183	61%
Europe	40,945	12%
Canada	24,026	7%
Latin America	30,502	4.8%
Total Number of Tourists	341,125	

Source: Belize Tourist Board.

situation could change, because it is impossible to stop everything. The new airport terminal can handle the huge influx of new flights from North America.

I'm no aviation expert, but I would expect flights from Europe to start soon. The Brits are the largest tourist group from Europe, but the Germans and the Dutch come in great numbers, as well. Some hotels are already posting prices in Euros. That means opportunity, since once those flights start Belize will be more accessible and more popular as a tourist destination and a place to invest and retire.

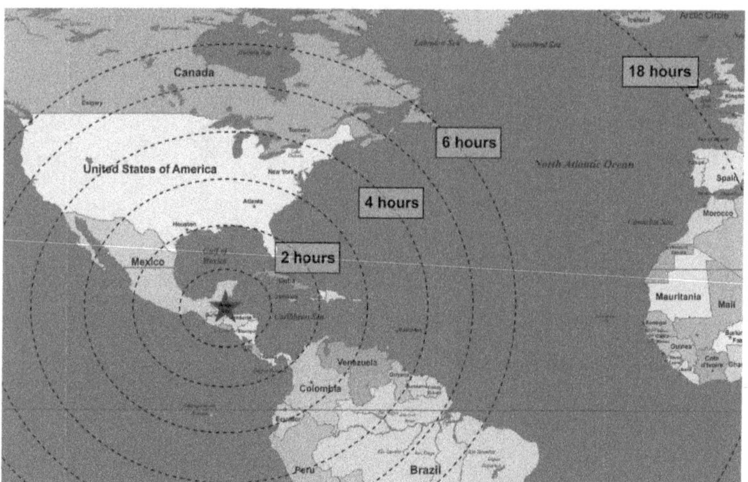

Flying times from Belize City.

Maya Island Air commuter planes connect to Mexico, Honduras, Guatemala, and Panama.

Being Eco-Friendly Pays

The best diving in the world in the azure waters of Belize.

Fishing flats.

- Coral reef- and mangrove-associated tourism contributes an estimated $200 million to the national economy, or 12 to 15 percent of GDP.
- Fishing is an important cultural tradition, as well as a safety net and livelihood for many coastal Belizeans.
- Economic benefits from reef- and mangrove-dependent fisheries is estimated at between $14 million and $16 million annually.
- Reefs and mangroves also protect coastal properties from erosion and wave-induced damage, providing an estimated $231 million to $347 million in avoided damages per year.

Source: World Resources Institute

Belize is a paradise for eco-tourists. Whether it's hiking in forests, snorkelling in the shallow waters off the cayes, or taking exotic treetop trips into the rainforest, eco-tourism is one of the country's unique attractions.

This book isn't a tourist guide. The reason I bring up all the natural beauty is because it enhances any investment here, as well as the joy of living in Belize.

Saving and Rebuilding the Mangroves

People sometimes sneer when they hear being green is good for business and produces business activity on its own. Robert Riley is an example of how cleaning up the environment benefits the ecology and the economy.

Riley lives near Cape Canaveral in Florida and travels the world restoring mangroves. He has worked on many continents and is now rebuilding coastal mangrove forests, as well as planting new mangroves to preserve existing coastal properties. I'll let him explain:

Sustainable Coastal Development in Belize

A major portion of the Belizean archipelago includes the forests and wetlands formed by the native mangrove trees. Mangroves are an indigenous species to Belize, as well as many tropical areas of the world, and a major contributor to the marine environment. The mangrove tree is a halophyte, a plant that thrives in salt water and the tidal areas of lagoons and estuaries. It has the ability to grow where no other tree can and is an active member of the coastal ecology.

Three species of mangroves are distributed along the Belize coastline and throughout the neighbouring Caribbean countries. The red mangrove is easily identified by its distinctive aerial roots, which suspend it over the water, thereby giving it extra support and providing protection for the water's edge. The black-and-white species do not have aerial roots, but are also well adapted to the intertidal zone. Buttonwood is a mangrove-type tree; all are important in forming coastal habitat.

The mangrove trees' coverage of coastal shorelines, coupled with the wetlands they create, provide a unique, irreplaceable habitat for many diverse species of birds, mammals, and fish. Mangroves preserve water quality by filtering and removing pollutants from coastal waters, thus promoting the health of economically important coral reefs and the associated tourist

There are hundreds of islands and cayes off the coast of Belize.

industry. Belize has one of the most diverse coral reef systems in the world, with the main types including fringing reefs along the coastline, the barrier reef along the continental shelf, and three offshore atoll reefs known as Lighthouse Reef, Glover's Atoll, and Turneffe Atoll. Belize has the longest barrier reef in the western hemisphere and is second only to the Great Barrier Reef of Australia.

The health of the Belizean reef system, which is threatened by various human activities, is critical to the tourist industry that makes up approximately 19 percent of the country's GDP. Over 25 percent of all jobs in Belize are tourism-driven or tourism-related.

Discovery of the importance of mangroves to the health of coral reefs worldwide has focused new attention toward mangrove reforestation. The mangrove tree is the foundation in a complex marine food chain and an integral part of the life cycle of many commercially important fish.

The Benefits of Mangroves

- basis of a complex marine food chain
- creation of breeding and nesting habitat
- establishment of restrictive impounds that offer protection for maturing offspring
- filtering and assimilating pollutants from upland runoff
- stabilization of bottom sediments and reduction of damage from the movement of tides
- water quality improvements
- protection of shorelines from storms and erosion

> Numerous species, whose continued existence depends on thriving mangroves, are endangered or threatened. It has been estimated that 75 percent of the game fish and 90 percent of the commercial species rely on the mangrove system.

Belize real-estate developers have teamed with eco-entrepreneur Robert Riley of the international environmental consulting firm mangrove.org for the design and implementation of sustainable coastal communities. Sustainable development ensures the well-being of both human and ecological components by integrating social and economic development with technology in mangrove reforestation.

Development and population growth will continue to have a negative impact on the mangrove habitat necessary to maintain the commercial and recreational fisheries of Belize. However, patented methods in mangrove reforestation invented by Mr. Riley are leading to more ecologically sound waterfront development practices.

The Barrier Reef

From the beach in San Pedro, you can see a long, white strip as the waves break on the coral barrier reef less than a mile offshore. This is especially dramatic at night. It's the second largest of its kind in the world, right after Australia's Great Barrier Reef. Though second in size to Australia's reef, the barrier reef that runs the entire length of Belize's Caribbean coast is the largest "living reef" in the world. Most other barrier reefs (such as the Great Barrier Reef) are made of dead coral. Belize's reef is alive with coral and divers are warned not to touch the reef because they might kill the coral.

The reef not only protects the community from large waves during storms, it's also a diver's and snorkeller's paradise; you can see — and if you dare, even touch — native sea life, such as sharks and rays, swishing through the magnificent coral.

Belize's unique barrier reef was named a World Heritage Site in 1996. The reef can be as far as twenty-five miles off the coast of Belize, but from San Pedro and Ambergris Caye it is just a few hundred yards away. It's hard to calculate the value of Belize's reef, but my friends at the tourist board tell me that almost half (45.6 percent) of all the tourists visit or view the barrier reef.

Diver with a turtle at Lighthouse Reef Atoll.

Wildlife

Belize's rainforest and its abundant wildlife are easily accessible. There are tours from San Pedro and other locations that can take you by boat into the jungle. Some clever Italian investors have built an upscale resort — Kanantik Reef and Jungle Resort — that includes everything eco, including tours of the jaguar reserve. It is easy to get to: it has its own private airstrip.

The jaguar is the largest cat in the Americas, protected in the Belize rainforest. The effort Belize has put into preserving its natural beauty pays off. When I

The jaguar is the largest cat in the Americas, protected in the Belize rainforest.

mentioned Belize to a friend's sixteen-year-old son, his first reaction was "That's where they have the jaguars." Well, it isn't the only place they have jaguars, but it is the largest nature preserve dedicated to the giant cat. A visitor has to be lucky to see one of the reclusive animals, but just wandering along the trail of the reserve, with its waterfalls and streams, is a fantastic experience.

Belize's natural beauty and abundance of wildlife creates business opportunities in things as unique as birdwatching. Some of the best birdwatching in the world is in Belize. Species such as the keel-billed toucan, the scarlet macaw, the harpy eagle, and the jabiru stork attract birders the way the reefs attract divers.

A couple from Cincinnati combined a humanitarian trip to Belize with birding. The husband, Dr. Michael Wood,

The keel-billed toucan, the national bird of Belize.

a cancer specialist, had been part of a Christian medical mission in rural Belize. He performed twenty-five operations while he was there. His wife, Sally, who has fifteen bird feeders outside their home in the United States, was there to help with the mission and to do some birding in her spare time. After four days in western Belize, near the border with Guatemala and Mexico, she was making notes in her bird diary, checking off the species she had seen against a Peterson bird guide.

"This is the southern edge of migration for many birds from North America. For example, the blue heron will be heading back north soon," she told us. But it was more than just the blue heron that caught her eye through her field telescope. "I saw 115 different types of birds and that includes fifty-nine new life birds. ['New life birds' is birding-speak for new birds to add to one's list of species seen at least once.] We saw everything from a little red-capped manakin to a jabiru stork. We were disappointed that we missed seeing the keel-billed toucan, the national bird of Belize."

Even the casual visitor, not just a dedicated birder, will be blown away by the variety of birdlife in Belize. The jungles are also home to five species of wildcats: the jaguar, the ocelot, the margay, the jaguarundi, and the puma, also known as the cougar. These spectacular animals are protected in areas that attract eco-tourists from around the world.

Cave tubing is a safe adventure sport. There are tours set up just an hour west of Belize City, at the bargain rate of US$50 a day. As one operator points out, this is an experience that is unique to Belize. There is no other Caribbean destination where you can float safely down a river in an inner tube.

Cruise ship off the coast of Belize.

At the other end of the spectrum are cruise ships. In the first edition of this book we predicted that cruise ship arrivals would pass one million. That happened in 2016, according to Manuel Heredia, the tourism minister.

"We are doing much better than before because we have better security and we have enhanced the whole area around the tourism village," he says. "There is a new cruise terminal in Harvest Caye, owned by Norwegian Cruise Line, two miles south of Placencia."

Honeymoon in Paradise

As I say, this book can't pretend to be a tourist guide, but knowing about business opportunities is helpful. The most romantic of these is the growing honeymoon tourism business in Belize. It presents a host of opportunities for the business person who might be looking for ideas to start a new enterprise in paradise.

"Honeymoon tourism is becoming very popular, not only on the island [Ambergris Caye], but in the interior part of Belize," says Tourism Minister Manuel Heredia. "We do a lot of advertising and over here Victoria House is becoming popular for honeymooners now, as well as weddings. Likewise, we have Rojo Lounge, which caters particularly to honeymooners."

Belize is small, but it packs a lot into a place that is a little less than two hundred miles from the north to the south and about seventy miles from the beaches of San Pedro in the east to the deep jungle of the Maya Mountains along the western border with Guatemala.

Because Belize squeezes so much into a compact country, the honeymooning couple can spend a day trekking in the jungle and that evening have dinner in a beachfront restaurant in San Pedro, Caye Caulker, or Placencia.

One evening, while having dinner at the Victoria House resort at the top of Ambergris Caye, I saw at least three young couples on their honeymoons. As we made small talk with them in the bar, one woman said how much she and her new husband enjoyed taking a boat ride from San Pedro to the deepest jungle. They had overnighted at a resort upriver and then seen some Mayan ruins the next day.

All of these excursions are made possible by the clever entrepreneurs who offer the services, from the boat operators who take people along the coasts and up deserted rivers, to the owners of boutique resorts. These are not big operations, but they are well-thought-out and, in many cases, owned by people who have brought their business smarts and business dreams here.

Belize is the kind of place where business opportunity abounds. Just like the real-estate market, Belize is a ground-floor opportunity for small- and medium-size businesses that aim to serve the tourism industry. The honeymoon market is a niche area, and one that captures the imagination. But there are other places where small enterprises can expand.

So think of the dreamy honeymoon couple sipping cocktails at sunset on Caye Caulker or scaling a Mayan ruin in the jungle; and what that should suggest is the opportunity that exists in Belize for any number of businesses. In spots throughout this book I am going to profile some success stories, big and small. The Pioneers chapter had a few of them, but there is one of my favourites coming up in the next chapter.

The Cayes of Belize

The cayes of Belize are unique in the Caribbean. They are sprinkled along Belize's 190-mile coastline from the largest, Ambergris Caye in the north, to isolated Blackbird Caye a few miles off the famous Great Blue Hole, all the way down to the Sapodilla Cayes, off the southern tip of the Placencia Peninsula. Maybe one of the best ways to see many of them is to rent a catamaran from one of the charter firms in San Pedro.

There are tiny spots like Hermit Caye, a 7.5-acre island that sold to a private buyer, to larger islands filled with life. Let me tell you about a few of them.

Caye Caulker is so laid-back you'll think you've fallen off the end of the earth. The main road is dirt, with modern condos on one side and street vendors on the other. It is now the second most popular tourist destination in Belize, capturing the title from Placencia. On a warm evening,

Caye Caulker: maybe the most laid-back place on earth.

people in bathing suits sit at a bar table, their feet in the water, sipping drinks, laughing, and listening to music.

Caye Caulker is a small coral island, eight miles long and never more than a mile wide. An unusual feature is that it is split in two by a channel, right where the bar is, and people, most of them young, hang around this spot, partying and forgetting about their worries and where they came from.

There is some debate about how the channel came to be, but the standard story is it was created when Caye Caulker, and all of Belize, was devastated by Hurricane Hattie in 1961. The legend says there was a trickle of water and locals dredged it out so canoes and then small fishing boats could take a shortcut from one side of the island to the other. Back then there were few tourists and Caye Caulker, like San Pedro, was a simple fishing village. How times have changed.

The Belize government has done some grooming of its own on Caye Caulker, says the minister of tourism, Manuel Heredia.

Relaxing in Caye Caulker

"There have been many improvements in Caye Caulker, in particular the nice beach we built there, since they never really had a nice beach so we built one and that really made a big difference," says the minister.

The sand on Caye Caulker is white coral, and reflects the sun in the daytime. At night the main street is alive with people walking, but stroll along the road beside the water and all of a sudden you are transported to a tropical nirvana. It is the kind of place that seduces people to stay forever, people like an Air France pilot or an Italian couple who found a way to live their dream.

On a winter afternoon by the dock at Caye Caulker hip tourists from Europe mix with what look like quaint leftovers from Woodstock. A bearded man in his sixties dressed in a bright, flowered shirt sells shrimp on the street from a small barbeque.

"I'm from New Jersey," he says, authenticating that statement with an accent you could cut with a knife. "I was born in the same hospital as Lou Costello [the comedian of Abbott and Costello]. Sure you won't have a shrimp?" This is perhaps an extreme example of how expats make a living in Belize.

In the centre of town is the cemetery, with old English names on the tombstones. It seems out of place, but just adds to the character of Caye Caulker. So do places such as the Rasta Pasta Rainforest Café, where locals and tourists enjoy spicy breakfasts or giant burritos. At the nearby Rainbow Grill and Bar, you can sit on a deck that projects into the water and watch a couple of fishermen spincast for snapper and barracuda. The side streets on Caye Caulker are quiet and peaceful. There are modern condos and beach houses here, at prices so low they would shock North Americans. "Caye Caulker is one of the great places in the world. It's bohemian and laid-back," said local businessman Simon Reardon-Smith. Then he joked, "I used to think my friends would come here just to see me, but it was the delights of Caye Caulker they were after."

Pasta Per Caso

The super-relaxed atmosphere of this sliver of paradise belies the fact that business is booming. Boutique hotels are popping up to serve the growing tourist numbers. There is also my favourite Italian restaurant, not just in Belize but anywhere. This is more than just a restaurant, but another business success story in Belize.

Armando and Anna Pau moved to Caye Caulker from Italy in February of 2013. "We had no plans," said Armando. In August of that first year

Armando and Anna Pau at their Caye Caulker restaurant.

in Belize the two of them opened a small restaurant on the main street of Caye Caulker with a simple seven-word philosophy: *Dinner Choices: Take it or Leave It,* posted inside the tiny restaurant. It's just a little more than 160 square feet, and on a hot June night, it is packed.

Their formula is simple, so simple that they only serve two pasta dishes: one vegetarian, one meat. Take it or leave it. Judging by the lineups outside the restaurant, the customers love it. He makes the pasta, from scratch, and she makes the sauce and runs the kitchen.

It is a love story with each other, and a love story with Belize, ending with success on this coral island.

"We met in Nigeria. I worked at the Italian embassy, Anna managed the catering administration for a large construction company," said Armando. He had worked in the airline business for twenty-four years before taking leave to work in Nigeria for a year.

He was born in Sardinia, but grew up in Verona. She came from Abruzzo on the Adriatic.

"When I returned to Italy, I could no longer endure the routine. In my job I felt like a number; professionally it was as if I had gone backwards fifteen years. As soon as I could, I would go back to visit Anna in Abruzzo."

Then he took a short holiday in Belize.

"I came here alone, and three days after I sent her a ticket – you have to come – I told her. After the first trip, there was a second, longer one, in the midst of acquiring a piece of land, leaving my job in aviation and the knowledge of having found a place in which to build something."

At first the plan was to produce and sell fresh pasta to the restaurants on the island and to San Pedro, as well. But when their friends tasted their cooking, plans changed.

"Our friends encouraged us to open a real restaurant; the very first night we served thirty-six people."

Armando says Belize offered him what Italy never could: the chance to open a restaurant. He says in Italy, the taxes, regulations, and jumping through political hoops would have doomed the project before it started. They are busy, working long hours, but they are proof that Belize is a place where you can start and run a business.

"Now when we travel, even in Italy, it is Caye Caulker that we call home," says Anna. "Let's go home, we'll say."

The colonial governors of British Honduras used to have beachfront mansions on Blackbird Caye, part of the Turneffe Atoll facing the Great Blue Hole. But those mansions were washed away long ago by violent hurricanes, before people learned to put up buildings that could withstand the elements.

The Turneffe Atoll is one of the first places where the British buccaneers took refuge when they came to Belize. Flying over, it is nothing but green. There is the occasional fishing camp built by adventurous locals, but for the most part it is uninhabited, a pristine green jewel sitting in the Caribbean Sea. It is as long as Barbados.

Along the edge of Blackbird Caye is a landing strip running parallel to the ocean. It must be one of the most beautiful places in the world to take a holiday. Well-furnished thatched huts right on the water offer the perfect place to get away from it all. Just a few hundred yards away is a dining hall with food cooked by an experienced chef. This is the kind of paradise that would cost thousands of dollars a day in the eastern Caribbean, but it can be had for a couple of hundred dollars a night at Blackbird Caye.

You can sit and read a book here, or dive. The reef that runs the length of Belize is even closer to shore here than it is in San Pedro. There is spectacular diving, and even a diving school where you can be certified. At the far end of the Caye, just past the Blackbird Caye Resort, is a world-famous oceanographic research station.

There is development occurring, and it is possible to buy property at this end of the atoll. But the developer and government alike are conscious of the delicate beauty of this place and are being careful to preserve what I think must be one of the most beautiful and unique slices of paradise on this planet. Just treat yourself to a few days there.

The entire Turneffe Atoll is 26,000 acres; it is not larger than Barbados, but it is longer. Blackbird Caye is 4,700 acres and of those, 3,000 acres are privately owned.

• • • • •

If you think you might have missed the boat, think again. There are entire islands and long stretches of remote islands still available in Belize. If you want to find a place to drop off the edge of the world for a while, this is it.

Opportunities for Medical Tourism in Belize

There is already a growing medical tourism market where smart doctors from other countries have set up to provide services that are superexpensive in North America and Europe. From plastic surgery to hip replacements, it's cheaper in Belize.

Since the growing retirement and expat community is not covered by state medicine in Belize, a large slice of the people living in the country at any one time, maybe 10 percent or more, can afford private health care and are willing to pay for it.

The Basics of Everyday Life

If you've never been to Belize before, don't worry about culture shock. While it is in many ways different from the United States and Canada, many things in daily life are pretty much the same.

Facts and Figures for Tourists

- Currency: U.S. dollars are accepted everywhere and people don't rip you off on the exchange rate. It's pretty simple: two Belize dollars equals one U.S. dollar.
- Credit cards: Almost all resorts accept the big two, Visa and MasterCard, and American Express is accepted in most locations.
- Banking: Modern ATMs are available in most populated areas. For day-to-day banking the system in Belize is comparable to that in North America, though, as with many things in Belize, it might move a little slower than you're used to.

- Electricity: The same as in Canada and the United States. Even the plugs are the same, so anything you bring from Canada and the United States will work in Belize. By the way, locals often refer to electricity as "current."
- Crime: This can be a problem in parts of Belize City. A well-publicized murder in the Cayo District was probably a love triangle. That can happen anywhere. San Pedro, the number one tourist destination, is remarkably safe and Danny Guerrero, the mayor of Ambergris Caye, wants to keep it that way. "My aim is to sell Belize as a safe destination. We work very closely with the police. We have a project putting solar lights on the beachfront. We started with eight and we have ordered twelve more and we are putting them in the dark areas so tourists can feel safe. The council is looking into putting solar lights in all our parks," says the mayor.
- Getting around: The longest flight in Belize is about an hour. In most cases you can get from point A to point B in fifteen minutes' flying time. Water taxis are everywhere. You can rent a car outside the tourist areas and there are tour guides and heavy-duty vehicles to take you into rough terrain. In San Pedro golf cart rentals are everywhere.
- Weights and measures: Miles, inches, and feet, just like the United States. Even though Belize is a former British colony, gasoline is sold in American, not imperial, gallons.

CHAPTER 12

EASY RETIREMENT IN BELIZE

MANY countries want to attract retiring baby boomers. Costa Rica did a good job attracting North Americans, but as with many other countries, from Switzerland to Uruguay, it is a place with too many rules. *International Living* wrote that "much of [Costa Rica's] appeal was lost in 1992 when the government rescinded most of the benefits of the famous *pensionado* program that, for thirty years, has attracted droves of expats."

Belize saw what was happening and improved on it. The Qualified Retirement Program of Belize was passed in 2000. It sets out the rules for people who want to retire, full- or part-time, in Belize. The program is one of those win-win situations: it's great for retirees and it creates jobs and wealth for the locals. The idea behind the plan is to help grow Belize's economy.

"We're dealing here with a small economy. For Belize to grow we have to bring in people with capital, expertise, and new technology. We have to realize we can't do it alone. And we have this vast amount of land, so much of it sitting idle," said a former cabinet minister.

Belize set out to attract a relatively affluent group of people by setting the bar for entry well above the country's average income. People who want to retire have to prove they have an annual income of US$2,000 a month, or US$24,000 a year. Not rich by American standards, but enough to ensure a really comfortable life in Belize. Obviously, most people retiring to Belize would have more capital and income than the minimum. There are no cumbersome regulations weighing down the retirees. Retirees have to be at least forty-five years old and promise to spend a month a year in the country. And that's it.

The Benefits

The Perks of Retirement in Belize

1. Bring in furniture, a car, a boat — even a plane — tax-free.
2. Pay no tax on your worldwide income.
3. Run your business from Belize.
4. Be close to "home" in the U.S. or Canada.

The retirement program allows you to bring in a car or light truck for your personal use without any tax or duty. You can also import household effects, furniture, and appliances (the electrical system is 110 volts, the same as in the United States and Canada), and a boat. There is no limit on the size of the boat, as long as it is for personal use and not for a business such as commercial fishing. You can even bring in a small, private aircraft. The maximum takeoff weight limit is 1,700 kilograms, (about 3,800 pounds), which easily accommodates such popular small planes as the Cessna 182.

Once someone qualifies for retirement, the rules apply to their spouse.

There are no income taxes for retirees and no tax on the investment income you bring into the country or on what's known as your worldwide income. If you want to operate your business, such as consulting, from Belize, you can do so easily, connecting to the rest of the world by internet and telephone. The income from that kind of operation in an International Business Company (IBC) is not taxed.

The exception is if you earn money in a regular job in Belize. Then you pay tax like every other citizen. Few retirees are faced with this problem.

There is modern health care in Belize, with medicare for the local population, but it does not apply to retirees. You have to buy insurance, as you would if you were spending time outside your home country. There are private clinics that provide excellent health care at affordable prices and that means cheap, by American standards.

Finally, Belize offers security for people seeking a new home. Although people don't often talk about it, Belizeans don't rip off newcomers. Belize City doesn't have teeming slums or shantytowns such as you see in Brazil, Jamaica, and other countries. Respect for property rights and the rule of law pays off.

Retirement in Belize: The Basics

Anyone over the age of forty-five with an income of at least $2,000 a month can retire in Belize.

You can conduct worldwide business tax-free: this includes professionals such as consultants. There are few rules, but you must reside there at least one month a year, which is no hardship. Commonwealth citizens can vote once they have established residency.

Many other places in Latin America and the Caribbean are plagued with the problem of squatters' rights. In theory there are squatters' rights in Belize, but in practice those rights are seldom exercised. The law in Belize states that in the case of private property, someone has to be in possession for twelve years and with government property it has to be thirty years of "undisturbed possession." So while squatters' rights exist in theory, in reality there are almost no instances of it. When you buy a property, you can be confident that there is no threat to your possession of it.

The Rules for Retiring in Belize:

1. All Qualified Retired Persons must adhere to the general procedures cited by the Customs Department for the clearing of all personal and household effects including "Mode of Transportation." (Household effects include furniture, a car, a boat, and even a small plane.)
2. Qualified Retired Persons are not allowed to seek employment or work for pay while in this program or in Belize. (Note: this does not apply to consulting or work that is essentially done remotely in another country.)
3. Qualified Retired Persons within this program must inform the Belize Tourism Board regarding any changes stated on the application form. Failure to do so may result in the revocation of the applicant's status.
4. Qualified Retired Persons must adhere to all existing laws of Belize, in addition to the Retired Persons (Incentives) (Amendment) Act, 2001.

5. All benefits provided by this program will be exclusively used by the Qualified Retired Persons and his or her dependents.
6. The Belize Tourism Board has the authority to carry out any investigation with respect to the validity of any document provided by the applicant under this program.
7. Participants within this program must inform the Belize Tourism Board prior to leaving the country indefinitely so that the assets purchased under this program can be liquidated. (Note: those assets refer to things such as the tax-free goods brought into the country by the retirees.)
8. All documents presented to the Belize Tourism Board become the property of the Board. (Note: these are things such as copies of bank statements and birth certificates.)
9. The applicant must not have any criminal matters with the law at the time of application.
10. Applicants must present a listing with all the necessary information with regards to his or her dependents. If the applicant has a dependent over eighteen and in school, then he or she must present a proof of enrolment from that institution.
11. Qualified Retired Persons must submit a yearly bank statement showing compliance with the financial requirements of the program. (Note: this refers to proving income of $2,000 a month.)
12. Qualified Retired Persons must spend an equivalent of one month in Belize annually to maintain their status as a Retiree Resident.

Source: Government of Belize website (www.belize.gov.bz/)

Visa Requirements

- All visitors must travel to Belize on a valid passport (non-expired). The passport must be valid for no less than six months after the intended period of stay in Belize.
  Note: Any person who is the holder of a valid United States of America multiple entry visa or a U.S. permanent residency card does *not* need a visa to enter Belize: such travellers are given a thirty-day tourist visa upon entry. Please call the consulate for further information.
- Cruise passengers: One-day cruise ship passengers do not require a visa for Belize.
- Work Visa: Visas for work, both paid and unpaid, are only issued in Belize before entry.

Requirements for Canadian Citizens to enter Belize:

Canadian citizens do not need visas for tourists or business visits of up to thirty days, but they must have onward or return air tickets for flights leaving within thirty days and proof of sufficient funds to maintain themselves while in Belize.

To stay longer than thirty days as a tourist (who may not do paid or unpaid work) an Extension of Stay application must be submitted while in Belize at any of the immigration offices. It is best to submit an application at least two to three days before the thirty-day period expires. The fee is BZ$50 for the first six months and BZ$100 thereafter.

An individual can apply for permanent residence after having paid one year of legal residence fees in Belize on a continuous basis.

Requirements for Canadian Residents who do not have a Canadian passport:

Note: Canadian citizens not residing in Canada must contact the Belize Embassy or Consulate closest to their place of residence.

Do I Need a Visa?

Nationals of the following countries *do not* require a visa to enter Belize as a tourist for a period of up to 30 days:

- Any person who is the holder of a valid United States of America multiple entry visa or a Permanent Residency Card (new)
- Citizens of the European Union member states (EU) and their dependent territories
- Citizens of the Caribbean Community Member States (CARICOM) with the exception of Haiti
- Citizens of the United States of America and dependent territories
- Citizens of Brazil, Colombia, Panama, Costa Rica, Chile, Guatemala, Iceland, Mexico, Norway, Switzerland, South Africa, Tunisia, and Uruguay
- Citizens of the Commonwealth Realms & Monarchies, and their dependent territories
- Citizens of the Commonwealth Republics, with the exception of the following: Bangladesh, Nauru, Cameroon, Pakistan, Chad, Sri Lanka, India, Mozambique, and some East African Countries

Nationals of all other countries *require* a visa to enter Belize.
*Visa requirements may change. Please check before travelling.

Other Belize Retirement Rules

Details can be found on the Belize tourism website (www.belizetourismboard.org/programs-events/retirement-program/). It is also available in French and German. Here are some highlights:

> The Qualified Retirement Program (QRP) was created to facilitate eligible persons who have met the income requirements to permanently live and retire and relax in Belize. These requirements include providing proof of permanent or consistent income from an investment both internationally or locally, retirement benefits, or

pension. Get ALL the facts about this program and discover how you can make this tranquil destination your next home. For more information contact Ms. Leannie Azueta — Licensing and QRP Officer at the Belize Tourism Board via email at leannie.azueta@belizetourismboard.org or [by phone at +501-227-2420, ext. 232].

Incentives

Any person who has been designated a Qualified Retired Person shall be entitled, on first entering Belize, to import his or her personal effects and an approved means of transportation free of all import duties and taxes.

A Qualified Retired Person shall be exempt from the payment of all taxes and duties on all income or receipts which accrue to him or her from a source outside of Belize whether that income is generated from work performed or from an investment.

Regulations

All privileges, exemptions and regulations herein included are governed by the Retired Persons (Incentives) (Amendment) Act, 2001 and the ACT will serve as the basis for all purposes of interpretation.

1. Personal Household Effects
   Qualified Retired Persons have one year from the date that they officially enter the program to import their personal and household effects free of duties and taxes as determined

by the Customs Department. Numerous entries are permitted within the one year period; however, your detailed master list of household and personal effects must be submitted to the Belize Tourism Board upon approval into the Program. After the year has elapsed, you will be subject to all duties and taxes under the Customs Department.

2. Transportation
   a. Motor Vehicle
      Qualified Retired Persons are strongly encouraged to procure a vehicle in Belize. However, we will facilitate duty and tax exemption on an imported vehicle.
   b. Light Aircraft
      A Qualified Retired Person is entitled to import a light aircraft less than 17,000 kg. A Qualified Retired Person is required to have a valid Private Pilot license to fly in Belize. This license can be obtained by passing the requirements set by the Civil Aviation Department. However, if the participant already has a valid pilot's license, that license only has to be validated by Civil Aviation Department in Belize.
   c. Boat
      Any vessel that is used for personal purposes and for pleasure will be accepted under this program.
3. Disposal of Duty Free Items
   If for whatever reason a Qualified Retired Person decides to sell, give away, lease, or otherwise dispose of the approved means

of transportation or personal effects to any person or entity within Belize, all duties and taxes must be paid by the qualified retiree to the proper authorities.

Qualified Retired Persons must note that only after 3 years and upon proof that the vehicle previously imported into Belize under the Program has been disposed of according to regulations, will another concession be granted to import a new transportation.

4. Offenses and Penalties

   Any person who knowingly makes any false declaration or entry in order to qualify for or renew any exemption or privilege granted under the Retired Persons (Incentives) (Amendment) Act, 2001 commits an offence and shall be liable on summary conviction to a fine not exceeding one thousand dollars.

5. Fee Structure

   a. A non-refundable application fee in the sum of US$150.00 payable to the Belize Tourism Board must be submitted with the application.
   b. A Program fee in the sum of US$1,000.00 payable to the Belize Tourism Board must be submitted upon acceptance into the Program.
   c. Upon acceptance into the Program a fee of US$200.00 must be paid to the Belize Tourism Board for the issuance of the Qualified Retired Person Residency Card. The QRP Card carries the information of your Biometric

Passport Page. [The QRP Card is to be scanned at least once by the Immigration Department, in order to link your membership record to the card and the Immigration Departments' System. The QRP Card can be used as a form of Identification/Immigration Status, if requested while moving within Belize. The QRP card cannot be used alone in crossing border points, but instead, is to be used in conjunction with your National Passport. Your passport will be stamped when travelling in and out, across border points.]

d. Each dependent is required to pay a Program Fee of US$750 to enter the Program.

   NOTE: All payments must be made payable to the Belize Tourism Board and be in the form of US cash, US bank draft or US cashier's check. Personal or company checks will not be accepted.

   Source: www.belizetourismboard.org/programs-events/retirement-program/#1490201475699-67d1052e-151a

Application Process

Each application for the Retirement Program will be processed by the Belize Tourism Board and forwarded to the Department of Immigration and Nationality. Persons interested in the program must submit completed applications to the

Belize Tourism Board with the following supporting documentation:

- Birth Certificate: A copy of a certificate for the applicant and each dependent
- Marriage Certificate: (if married and spouse is a dependent)
- Authentic Police Record: An authentic police record from the applicant's last place of residency issued within one month prior to this application
- Passport: Clear copies of complete passport (including all blank pages) of applicant and all dependents that have been certified by a Notary Public. The copies must have the passport number, name of principal, number of pages, and the seal or stamp of the Notary Public
- Proof of Income: (a.) An official statement from a bank or financial institution certifying that the applicant is the recipient of a pension or annuity of a minimum of Two Thousand United States Dollars (US$2,000) per month
- Medical Examination: Applicants should undergo a complete medical examination including an AIDS test. A copy of the medical certificate must be attached to the application
- Photos: Four front- and four side passport-size photographs that have been taken recently of applicant and dependents

Source: www.ambergriscaye.com/economics/retireNbelize.html

CHAPTER 13

OTHER OPPORTUNITIES FOR THE NEWCOMER

IT'S inevitable. Some of the people who retire to Belize will get restless, take a look around, and ask themselves, "What kind of business can I get into?"

It's happening already; indeed, most of the entrepreneurs in San Pedro are expats, people who have moved to Belize. Their businesses vary: an ice cream store, a pizza place, and golf cart, catamaran, and personal watercraft rentals. Almost all the small resorts I know of are run by people who have been attracted to Belize. There is Beth Clifford from the state of Maine at Mahogany Bay, Toshiya Tsujimoto from Japan, and Lindsey Hackston from England. There are people like German/Canadian Gabriel Kirchberger running rental properties on Costa del Sol, and Zubair Kazi from India and Los Angeles running a huge shrimp farm. Everywhere you look, there is a clever entrepreneur doing well in Belize.

I suggest you stick with what you know. The Belizean tax and business rules make it easy for you to run your consulting or other small personal business from Belize. The government has also set up Export Processing Zones, which are in effect tax-free zones to allow foreign businesses to flourish, particularly in manufacturing; however, they can also include service industries.

The Export Processing Zones are a potential bonanza for an outsider to do business in. In effect it means that you, as a business person, have your own country within Belize, in terms of import/export duties. Say you want to open a shrimp farm. You carve out a piece of land and all the imports and exports involved with that business are in a kind of free-trade zone.

The Export Processing Zones can be anywhere; there is no part of the country where they are not welcome. Of course, the business has to meet certain criteria (see the sidebar below for more information), but Belize is pretty liberal in this regard.

This is a win-win for the country and for the business owner.

The Commercial Free Zone is a geographic free-trade zone that everyone calls the Corozal Free Trade Zone. It is in the northern part of Belize right over the border from the town of Chetumal, the capital of the Mexican state of Quintana Roo. The concept

Economic Incentives

Corozal Free Trade Zone:

- Import material for business duty-free
- Export goods tax-free
- Tax-free holidays
- Last bastion of wild-west free enterprise

Beltraide:

- A website with extensive details of the Export Processing Zones and other incentives for business – Belize Trade and Investment Development Service: www.belizeinvest.org.bz

is that businesses locate there, and can import goods duty-free for manufacturing and resale. The Corozal Free Trade Zone is a great place for many small- to medium-sized businesses. It costs $5,000 to register as a retail business here, in addition to a $1,000 annual licence fee. Only foreigners can shop here, which includes Mexicans, vacationers, and Qualified Retired Persons. Belizean citizens are not allowed. You can buy cheap gasoline and diesel fuel, groceries, and household goods, including tools, liquor, shoes, and quality goods.

Any M.B.A. student who wants to study free trade should use the Corozal zone as a case study. It's a modern example of what free trade zones were 150 years ago in Hong Kong. It is the true essence of a free market and the free flow of capital and goods. The Corozal zone feels a bit like the Wild West: it's certainly free enterprise at its best.

Export-Import (2006)

Exports: sugar, bananas, citrus, clothing, fish products, molasses, wood.

Imports: machinery and transport equipment, manufactured good, fuels, chemicals, pharmaceuticals, food, beverages, tobacco.

Export to:	**%**	**Imports from:**	**%**
United States	28%	United States	30.6%
United Kingdom	18.8%	Mexico	14.1%
Thailand	5.7%	Cuba	8.4%
Côte d'Ivoire	5.2%	Guatemala	7.8%
Finland	4.1%	China	4.2%
Jamaica	4.1%		

Setting up a new business is one of the business opportunities available in Belize but there are other possibilities, including investing in established industries. I have listed some of the major ones below.

Agriculture

The mainstay of Belize's modern economy is tourism now, but its traditional agricultural trade hasn't disappeared. Sugar and bananas are important exports, as are new manufactured goods such as clothing. This trade offers exciting investment opportunities.

Citrus fruits are the number one export, followed by bananas. While tourism is ahead of individual agricultural commodities, including citrus, if you add up all the exports, farming is still the number one business in Belize.

The Mennonite settlement of Spanish Lookout in the Cayo District is one of Belize's prime food-growing areas.

Belize's geography and climate make it an agricultural haven. "Farming and livestock production employ approximately 23,000 people in Belize (a fifth of the employed population)," said an in-depth report on agriculture in Belize released in June of 2017 by the Inter-American Development Bank.

The four big products are oranges, poultry, sugar cane, and bananas. All of them are "… highly export oriented," in the words of the report.

The Mennonites who came to Belize from Canada a couple of generations ago now dominate farming in many areas of Belize. One of their settlements is a few miles outside San Ignacio. The blond, light-skinned settlers stand out in their horse-drawn carts and old-fashioned clothes. Don't be fooled. The Mennonites of Belize are responsible for building — though not running — many of the resorts in the area and bring old-world craftsmanship to many of the local buildings.

The Banana Belt

Belize is the perfect place to grow just about anything, with its ideal combination of sun and rain. It has attracted farmers from the Mennonites, who supply a huge percentage of the country's daily food needs, to immigrants from Iran and India who feed world markets for bananas and shrimp.

Eugene Zabaneh owns an 1,180-acre banana plantation in southern Belize. His father was born in Iran and came to Belize with his wife from El Salvador and started a small citrus farm. Eugene is an amazing entrepreneur, who has grown the small citrus operation into

Eugene Zabaneh on his banana plantation.

a major agricultural holding. As you will read elsewhere in this book, he also owns Maya Island Air, and commutes between his plantation and his office at Belize City Municipal Airport in less time than most big city drivers take to commute to work.

The first thing a visitor to a banana plantation notices is that all the bananas are wrapped in blue bags, used to protect the fruit from insects, among other things.

"You'll notice there are a lot of holes in the blue bag and that's for ventilation purposes, which accelerates the growth and the quality of the fruit," says Felipe Magana, a graduate agronomist who is the manager of the plantation. "It takes anywhere between sixty-three days and ninety-one days to be ready for cutting and shipping."

Eugene and Felipe lead a visitor through the process. After they are chopped from the tree, the large bunches

Agricultural exports.

of bananas are carried to a cable system for transportation to the packing house. There is a network of cables, called cableways, through the plantation, and no banana plant is more than one hundred feet from a cable line. Growing bananas is a labour-intensive process.

At the packing house the bananas are cleaned and packed into boxes, all weighing at least forty pounds, each box marked for Fyffes, the Irish company that buys all the bananas from this plantation. They are shipped directly to a nearby port, then make the trip across the Atlantic. Just about all the bananas in Ireland come from Belize, though others from Eugene Zabaneh's plantation make it to the United Kingdom.

"We cut the fruit between the ages of sixty-three and ninety-one days and after we cut it, it's processed in the packing shed, sent to the port, and from there it takes about eleven or twelve days at sea until it reaches its destination," says Eugene. "So from the time someone swings a machete at the banana plant, it's taken anywhere from fifteen to twenty-one days before someone is eating one of our bananas in Dublin or London."

Eugene's family started in the citrus industry and is still active. It, too, is a big contributor to Belize's economy.

Shrimp

Zubair Kazi came to the United States as a young man in 1969 and started work in a Kentucky Fried Chicken outlet. Within no time he owned a franchise. After several years he owned more than three hundred franchises. Today he owns around one hundred. His main interest now is medical research, through a company that manufactures a machine called Artemis, that diagnoses prostate cancer.

An incredibly successful businessman already, Zubair Kazi first came to Belize not to make more money but as a tourist. "I am from India where it's very tropical and a friend called me from Belize and said that if I was looking for a place like that, Belize is the best he knew of. So I just went there and happened to see this property on my first trip," said Kazi (many of his close friends call him by his last name). "Within twenty-four hours we shook hands and made the deal on this shrimp property."

Kazi finds it relaxing living and working in Belize. The British tradition reminds him of his childhood home in India. He says if you want to do business in Belize, you have to adjust to the local culture.

"The total population is only 380,000 people and everybody knows what others are doing and it's good not to get in anybody's way. I never had a problem because I approached everybody independently. You have to be respectful, respect what they need and what their thought process is and work accordingly and give them time to make things happen," he says.

Paradise Shrimp Farm has 3,600 acres and is capable of producing and processing ten million pounds of shrimp a year, though five million pounds was the largest crop so far. It is frozen and shipped to the United States, Mexico, Jamaica, Trinidad, and other places.

Fish farming is big business in Belize. These aerated ponds belong to Belize Aquaculture Ltd., on the mainland west of Paradise Shrimp Farm.

Lumber

Even before agriculture developed in Belize, lumber was the basis for the country's early economy. It still has a role today, but many people, including me, think a tree standing in the rainforest can produce more money in tourist dollars than it can sawed up into planks. As I mentioned, there are tree plantations with far-sighted entrepreneurs planting forests of teak and mahogany. The payback period is twenty years in the case of teak, twenty-five years with mahogany. The natural forests, and even the plantations, mean wildlife is left undisturbed.

Oil

Belize is an oil-producing country, though on a small scale. That's fine, since it is a small country. Some things have changed since I wrote the first edition of this book. Production peaked a few years ago, but the reserves are still there and Belize Natural Energy (BNE) is using modern technology — not fracking — to get more oil and gas out of the ground.

"We are the only oil-producing company in Belize," says Susan Morrice, co-founder and chairperson of BNE, and another example of a highly skilled person doing business in Belize. "In an era of sustained lower oil prices, Belize Natural Energy has survived and is thriving at a time when over 70 percent of oil companies in the U.S. have closed their doors."

Ms. Morrice splits her time between Denver and Belize. She is a trained geologist who graduated from

Trinity College, Dublin, in Ireland, one of the few women in her field at the time.

"I fell in love with Belize thirty-five years ago, with the people and the beauty of the place," says Ms. Morrice. "That is what has given me such passion and a deeper meaning to pursue this."

Before she, and her Belizean partner Mike Usher, and a group of mainly Irish investors discovered oil in 2005, there had been fifty dry wells drilled over fifty years. No one believed there was oil.

"We hit the very first oil discovery in Belize on the very first well we drilled. Can you imagine — we had five hundred thousand acres and we selected a site the size of a large dinner plate. Talk about finding a needle in a haystack. Some people said it was the luck of the Irish, but when they heard it was on the exact day one year later after the sudden death of Mike Usher they realized it was about something bigger than ourselves.

"Mike died on 24 June 2004 and we named our first well the Mike Usher 1. We hit the oil on 24 June 2005, a year to the day after he died," says Ms. Morrice. "It was against all odds; I mean there is just no way in the oil business when you drill your first wildcat that you ever hit oil."

Now her firm, Belize Natural Energy, is drilling in a new field called Never Delay near the capital, Belmopan.

"It's shallow and it's more challenging. We are using an American collection system to draw out the oil from each individual oil well while we are working with tapping into a greater fracture system," says Ms. Morrice.

BNE spent millions of dollars on infrastructure to access its drill sites. Some of it is being used by the public. The firm designed and built the new roundabout (traffic circle) going into Belmopan, which is spectacular.

BNE production facility, Spanish Lookout.

"It has the tallest flagpole in all of Belize with the largest flag. It's beautiful, with water fountains changing colour at night," says Ms. Morrice.

In addition to infrastructure, BNE, in partnership with the Government of Belize, has the BNE Trust, which has invested more than BZ$8 million to provide over a thousand scholarships for students from Belize.

Since oil was discovered in Belize in 2005 it has exported eleven million barrels of oil to refineries in the United States and around the world.

"That is a tremendous amount in revenue," says Bhoj Raj Choudhary, a petroleum engineer from Calgary. His firm, Fire Creek Resources, is working with BNE to use a patented technique to extract more oil and gas from the Never Delay field.

The oil discovery has helped transform the country's economy, because it has earned the government so much money. For every dollar of revenue from the oil fields, fifty-five cents goes to the public treasury.

"When it was five thousand barrels a day it was the main contributor as far as taxes and royalties to the Belize government. BNE, at that point, was the single largest contributor, by a large margin, to government revenue," says Mr. Choudhary. "If we explore more with further investment and we reach ten thousand barrels a day, which is possible, those sorts of numbers can come back again."

The oil discovery has made a huge positive change to Belize's balance of payments and that in turn has made the whole country richer.

Five thousand barrels a day may not sound like much, but as the price of oil spent most of the time from 2008 to 2014 hovering around US$100 a barrel it's an astounding windfall for a small country.

Mr. Choudhary feels there is a lot of potential, in particular in the new field near Belmopan.

"Belize's oil fields are close to Mexico. It's part of the same basin that Mexico has where all of the oil deposits have occurred for millions of years," says Mr. Choudhary.

Belize is right next door to Guatemala and Mexico, which have hundreds of millions of barrels of oil. There are estimates that BNE has fifteen million to twenty million barrels in producible oil reserves. Not a substantial amount on a world scale, but for a country with the population of Tampa, Florida, it's huge.

"The large portion of the oil that is going to be discovered in Belize is going to be technically challenging to recover. It's just underexplored, so far," says Choudhary.

Seventy percent of Belize's crude oil is shipped to refineries in the United States. The rest is used in Belize. The oil is so "light" coming out of the ground that it can be used to run diesel generators — and even some Mennonite tractors. BNE produces its own electricity for its sites from the crude oil.

In addition, BNE produces cooking gas domestically.

"We produce propane and butane, which is cooking gas. We generate electricity for our facilities, so it saves our costs but there is the potential to bring electricity to the local grid, depending on how much gas we find at Never Delay field," says Susan Morrice.

Oil in Belize is truly the icing on the cake. It will have an even more dramatic impact on the country if the new exploration techniques yield higher output.

"Even a small oil discovery has a huge effect on a small economy," says an American-trained economist working in Belize. "We have a billion-dollar economy, so that oil discovery made a huge difference."

But the real natural resource of Belize is the people. This is exemplified by the fact that BNE/Belize has become a global beacon, winning in 2017, at a ceremony in London, England, the Global Getenergy Award in the "Localisation" category, which is defined as "[Recognizing] the contribution of a company in supporting local education and supply chain capacity building."

Susan Morrice.

The Belize firm won against fifty other countries, and the final three included Canada and Oman. The award will undoubtedly attract more attention and investment to Belize.

The dynamic Susan Morrice can take a lot of the credit.

Electricity

Belize has a modern electrical grid that is constantly expanding. Belize Electricity Limited (BEL) is the primary distributor of electricity in Belize. Aggregate energy sold was approximately 541 gigawatt hours (GWh) in 2016. The company served a customer base of 90,635 accounts or 71,989 customers, with a peak power demand of approximately 96 megawatts (MW) during the year.

BEL's national electricity grid connects all major municipalities (load centres), except for Caye Caulker, with approximately 1,875 miles of transmission and primary distribution lines. The grid is primarily supplied by local independent power producers (IPP) utilizing hydroelectricity, biomass, petroleum, and solar energy sources, and is secured and stabilized by the interconnection with Mexico. BEL also operates a gas turbine plant as a standby plant for energy security and reliability.

The Government of Belize is the largest shareholder in BEL, with direct ownership of 32.6 percent interest in the company. The Social Security Board also owns 31.2 percent interest in the company, so that the public-sector interest amounts to 63.8 percent. Fortis Inc. owns 33.3 percent, and over 1,500 small shareholders own the remaining 2.9 percent interest in ordinary shares.

Several years ago I laid an underwater cable across the lagoon to bring power to Costa de Sol from San Pedro. The cable can handle five megawatts of load to power everything there now and handle future growth. All the electrical cabling on Costa de Sol is to be buried, so there won't be a power line in sight; just a few discreet power boxes, easily hidden by some greenery.

The Sun, the Wind, and Green Belize

Once upon a time solar panels were so expensive they were used only to power spaceships. Now technology and modern manufacturing techniques have reduced the cost of solar so that it is cheaper than the grid in many places, including Belize. Nowhere is that truer than on Costa del Sol. Electricity is expensive. The cost of a kilowatt hour in Belize is roughly the same as in New York City, but half that of Denmark and many other European countries. Solar and wind make sense on sunny Costa del Sol, where there is often a light, warm wind, enough to generate power.

"The potential for renewable energy on Costa del Sol, and for that matter all of Belize, is huge. You could run the entire island of San Pedro, as well as Belize, from renewable energy sources," says Jaspal Deol, an electrical engineer registered in California who spends time in Belize and is working with property owners on Costa del Sol to develop alternative energy strategies.

"Solar is a better solution but wind is also a possibility for the simple reason that if you integrate both of them it actually makes more sense."

One property owner on my island is installing solar for both electricity and to run his small desalination plant that turns salt water into fresh. One of his problems is that the people who rent his beautiful houses come from the United States, and especially Canada, where electricity is relatively cheap.

"They take long showers, sometimes more than once a day. It's what they are used to and it takes a lot of energy. Solar saves me a lot of money," says Gabriel Kirchberger, who rents out his luxury properties on Costa del Sol. "With the sun here it is a no-brainer."

Jaspal Deol plans an array of solar panels that track the sun east to west as it moves across the sky. If the solar is linked to a small wind generator, there would have to be some reliance on the electrical grid only at night. Mr. Kirchberger has just bought Brahma Blue, a four-storey condo building next door to his existing properties. Eventually Mr. Deol sees servicing his entire group of buildings with a thirty-five-kilowatt array of solar panels.

What is the payback period? The answer is amazing.

"About ten to twelve months."

This is all done without government incentives. The market is driving the conversion to renewables, with the falling price of solar panels and increasingly inexpensive storage options, such as batteries that can charge in the daytime and provide much of the power needed at night. In the not-too-distant future I see Costa del Sol as a green island, totally run on renewables. The government of Belize is thinking about these things as well.

"At this point the government is looking into alternative energy," says cabinet minister Manuel Heredia. "But we already have a factory generating electricity using the waste products from sugar cane."

Aviation

The shortest commercial flight in the western hemisphere is in Belize: three minutes and forty-eight seconds from takeoff to touchdown from Belize international airport to Belize City Municipal. Belize may be a small, emerging market country, but it has an aviation infrastructure second to none.

According to the minister of civil aviation, the number of flights per day in Belize can range from zero to only thirty-four. Despite the low number of flights, there are nine commercial airports in Belize: the two serving Belize City, mentioned above; the capital city, Belmopan; Placencia in the south; Dangriga; Caye

Caulker; San Pedro, the busiest after the international airport; Orange Walk; and Corozal. In addition, there are several private airfields serving resorts, including Kanantik, and two others, one near San Ignacio, the other serving Blackbird Caye, and there will soon be a small strip serving my island, Costa del Sol.

There are nine international airlines flying into Philip S.W. Goldson International in Belize: American Airlines, United, Delta, JetBlue, and Southwest from the United States; Air Canada and WestJet from Canada; Copa from Panama; and Avianca from Colombia.

The new terminal at Belize international is like a pressure valve, as the old facility was full to overflowing with the increase of visitors and retirees.

There is a private international airport already built at Placencia, an ambitious undertaking.

"The runway has been completed but the terminal has yet to be done in the south of Belize close to Placencia," said Manuel Heredia, Belize's minister of tourism and civil aviation in 2017.

The airport in Placencia is completely privately financed. In a conversation with Minister Heredia, we asked if the government had any objections to a private airfield big enough to handle international-sized aircraft.

"If you take a look at what we have with Philip Goldson, it's a concession to a group for about ten years now to the Belize Airport Concession Company. The terminal was built by the government, then the concession granted to this company. The new (Belize International) terminal is being built by the same concession company," said Mr. Heredia.

Perhaps the most exciting aviation development is the plans for an international airport at the northern end of Ambergris Caye. Until recently, the rumours of a new international airfield there were just that, only rumours. There is real progress toward a development that will open up a huge area. The minister confirms the site will be about fifteen miles north of the town of San Pedro.

"We have two hundred acres reserved for the international airport, which is supposed to be named Efrain Guerrero International Airport, after one of the pioneers of our party on the island," said the minister. "An American group is partnering with us to do the runway again under a certain contractual agreement."

As yet it is unclear just when construction will start, but the runway would be the longest in Belize, at 12,500 feet. At first the airfield would be available for charter flights and private aircraft.

"It's a three-point investment that they want to do for it to be feasible. The airport by itself would not be feasible. They are trying to get additional lands around that area so that there can be an EEZ, an Exclusive Economic Zone, similar to Corozal and where they can have two or three brand-name hotels," said Mr. Heredia.

Such an airport would open up huge swathes of undeveloped land in the north end of the island. It would mean direct access to San Pedro and, of course, to Costa del Sol property. There is already a new road partway to where the airport would be, and a number of boutique hotels have been developed there, including a number of high-end condo developments.

The airport at Caye Caulker has been dramatically improved, with a 3,000-foot runway installed in 2017 (it was 2,500 feet) that was also widened. Caye Caulker needed the upgrade. The new airfield has landing lights. The pilot alerts the field five minutes ahead of landing and the airstrip is lit, extending the daily use of the Caye Caulker airstrip. As you will read elsewhere in this book, the island just a few miles off San Pedro is now the second most popular tourist destination in the country.

The airport at Placencia (not the unopened international but the local) is the next to be upgraded, also with landing lights and an extended runway.

The Belize City Municipal Airport is totally new, with the two local airlines paying for the renovation. The runway is now 3,500 feet, it has been doubled in width to fifty feet, and there is a separate taxiway. The new terminal building has a comfortable, air-conditioned waiting room and free Wi-Fi. It is extremely comfortable for a small airfield.

At San Pedro, Tropic Air opened a new terminal several years ago and Maya Island Air has a new terminal on the other side of the arrival apron.

"The international market has grown by about 38 percent over the past three years and we are still improving those numbers," said Eugene Zabaneh, the owner of

The average flight time in Belize is twelve minutes.

Maya Island Air Fast Facts

- Average flight time: twelve minutes
- Capacity from Belize international: 100 percent
- Busiest run: Belize international to San Pedro
- Airports served: nine in Belize, one in Guatemala
- Convenient link from international flights to Mexico
- Operates STOL (Short takeoff and landing) Aircraft

Maya Island Air, in mid-2017. "We are presently putting in a terminal in San Pedro for the flights that come in from international points. Right now, we are refreshing our fleet with four new fourteen-passenger Caravan EX models, which are the latest Cessna manufactures."

The influx of tourists to Belize is driving growth in the aviation sector, as Eugene Zabaneh notes.

"Right now, our international passengers make up about 65 percent of our total passenger load with San Pedro being the busiest. Maya does twelve trips, so does Tropic Air." Imagine, twenty-four scheduled trips from Belize City to San Pedro daily.

In Central America and the Caribbean, Belize is the country that boasts the best domestic service. "Our airline is fifty years old and has had no fatal accidents," says one of its directors.

Gambling

Belize has made it easy for entrepreneurs to get into the casino business. The government has placed some sensible restrictions: casinos are for tourists and foreigners, not locals. A casino must be built around a resort, but the resort needn't be huge; a resort must have a minimum of fifty rooms to qualify for a casino licence. An example is Princess Casinos, owned and operated by the Turkish entrepreneur Sudi Özkan and his family. Their largest operation is the Ramada Belize City Princess Hotel.

Call Centres

Other business ventures in Belize include call centres; indeed, some have already started benefiting from the English-speaking workforce and taking advantage of the time zone. Belize is on Central Standard Time (CST), which is the same as Chicago and the heartland of the United States. It is just an hour behind New York (EST), two hours ahead of Los Angeles (PST), and six hours off London time (GMT).

CHAPTER 14

THE LAST WORD

BELIZE is an affordable paradise, and it appeals to a wide cross-section of people.

The beauty of the country and the tropical climate are the big draws for many of us. Diving and fishing still draw people, as does the barrier reef, the second longest in the world. Mayan ruins are archaeological wonders that match any pre-Columbian architecture in Central America.

For investors looking for a safe and attractive place for their money, Belize offers an unbeatable range of opportunities, from brand-name hotels to luxury condos for rental to beachfront properties.

Retiring to Belize is still as attractive as it ever was, too. Again, the real estate is attractive and affordable. Also, the rules are simple: if you can prove that you have US$2,000 a month in income you are given just about all the rights of a Belize citizen if you move to the country. You are allowed to bring in a car, household goods, a boat, even a small private aircraft, all duty-free.

I said at the start of this book that I told you so. Well, I am saying it again. Belize has prices you will never find in the Caribbean; it is English-speaking, with a rule of law and real-estate practices the same as you find in

Canada and the United States. It is a peaceful democracy with no history of civil unrest, unlike its neighbours.

Affordable real estate is not the only attraction, of course.

Tourism is a very important part of Belize's economy these days, and it offers tremendous opportunities for investors. Caye Caulker is now the number two tourist destination in the country after Ambergris Caye. It is still a laid-back oasis in a scrambled world, but it has new hotels, opportunities for development, and is a retirement paradise. An Italian couple has opened one of the most popular restaurants on Caye Caulker, a classic example of the business opportunities available across Belize.

On Ambergris Caye there is new development in the north. Boutique hotels and new condos along the beach facing the Caribbean are slowly filling a once empty area north of the bridge going out of San Pedro. There is still lots of vacant land ready for development, though, and friends of mine from the Los Angeles area just made an investment there.

There is a real chance of a private group building an international airport at the north end of Ambergris Caye. Imagine what that is going to do to the north end. Same story at Placencia in the south, where an entrepreneur has actually built an international airport. It isn't open at the time of writing, but it is there. As they say, build it and they will come.

My own piece of paradise, Costa del Sol, is developing into a cluster of luxury buildings with a unique view of nearby San Pedro, and, facing the other way, the empty expanse of Chetumal Bay. The last year has seen newcomers buying lots and long-time residents expanding their holdings. There are plans for other developments near Costa del Sol and the section I call the Platinum Coast.

At the southern end of Ambergris Caye there is real development that even someone as enthusiastic as I am did not foresee at the start of this decade. Mahogany Bay is an imaginative development that has a micro-village at its centre. There's a salon where you can get a haircut or a mani-pedi; there's also a coffee shop, sushi restaurant, spa, and hotel, one with a difference. La Sirene is a high-end residential development at the extreme southern tip of the island.

All of this is anchored to Victoria House, the first prime property in the area. An understated luxury hotel operated to the highest standards. The two Texans who founded Victoria House are examples of how imagination and hard work can build a successful business in Belize. Those two men don't live here all the time, but that is true about a lot of people who run businesses here. The new airline connections make it easier; for the first time I can now fly direct from my home in Calgary, Alberta, to Belize.

The surge in tourism, brought on by the huge increase in flights from the United States, Canada, and Latin America, has caused some strains on infrastructure, but that has been addressed with the new terminal at Belize City international. Travelling within the country has also been made easier. Once people get to the Belize City airport, almost all of them want to head out to other small airfields that make Belize so accessible. Those, too, are being upgraded. Belize City Municipal has a longer, wider runway, and a new terminal. By the time you read this Caye Caulker's airfield will be upgraded, in time to welcome more visitors.

Tourism is not the only opportunity for the entrepreneur in Belize, though. Other industries — agriculture, energy, call centres — also have potential.

In this edition of the book we have profiled a wide cross-section of successful business people, men and women, who operate viable businesses in Belize. These are real people working day-to-day and making a success of their lives. Many are in the early stages of retirement, others are young and have picked the country as a place to live and work.

Not only are there great investment and real-estate opportunities in Belize, there is also a very supportive business environment. Investors and retirees are able to benefit from a stable and open banking system and a number of well-developed government programs and rules. International banks, so called because they deal with people from outside the country, specialize in financing real-estate purchases in Belize, whether for an investment property or a place to retire. There are also government structures to help the entrepreneur in Belize, in particular the International Business Company, or IBC. That helps someone run a global business from Belize, and it doesn't have to be a large corporation: it can be something like a consultancy.

Natural beauty; great weather; affordable real estate; a strong economy with opportunities in tourism, agriculture, and other areas; a stable government; and a supportive business environment — Belize has it all.

Finding Belize changed my life. It can do the same for you.

ACKNOWLEDGEMENTS

I would like to thank the Belize Tourism Board. Its staff went beyond providing regular help with the writing of this book. For one thing, they answer the phone, a rarity in this day and age. The BTB's stock photos and statistical information permeate this book.

Karen Bevans runs the Belize Tourism Board and the co-operation and culture of the place starts with her. Along with running the BTB, Mrs. Bevans's talent has been recognized outside Belize. In 2016 she was elected Vice Chairman for the Board of Directors of the Caribbean Tourism Organization.

Karen and her team use the latest statistical and demographic information to attract tourists from North America, Britain, and Europe. The result: the surge in tourism that is the driver of Belize's economy.

APPENDICES

APPENDIX A
RESOURCES

Government Contacts

Government of Belize website: www.belize.gov.bz

Belize Tourism Board
64 Regent Street
Belize City, Belize
Tel: +501-227-2420
Fax: +501-227-2423
Email: info@belizetourismboard.org
Website: http://travelbelize.org

Banking

Domestic

Atlantic Bank Limited
Freetown Road
Belize City, Belize
Tel: + 501-223-4123

Bank of Nova Scotia
Albert Street
Belize City, Belize
Tel: +501-227-7027

Belize Bank Limited
Market Square
Belize City, Belize
Tel: + 501-227-7132

Heritage Bank of Belize (formerly Alliance Bank)
Princess Margaret Drive
Belize City, Belize
Tel: + 501-223-6111

International (source: Central Bank of Belize)

International banks licensed in Belize with an "A" Class — Unrestricted licence

Atlantic International Bank Limited
Withfield Tower, 2nd Floor
4792 Coney Drive
P.O. Box 1811
Belize City, Belize
Tel: +501-223-3152 or +501-223-5366

Belize Bank International Limited
The Matalon Business Center
Coney Drive, 2nd Floor
P.O. Box 364
Belize City, Belize
Tele: +501-227-0697 or +501-227-1548

Caye International Bank Ltd.
P.O. Box 11
Coconut Drive, San Pedro
San Pedro Ambergris Caye, Belize
Tel: +501-226-2388 or +501-226-2383

Choice Bank Limited
Power Point Building
Ground Floor
Corner Hudson Street and Marine Parade Boulevard
P.O. Box 2494
Belize City, Belize
Tel: +501-223-6850 or +501-223-6851

Heritage International Bank & Trust Limited
106 Princess Margaret Drive
Belize City, Belize
Tel: +501-223-6783 or +501-223-6784

International banks licensed in Belize with a "B" Class — Restricted licence

Market Street Bank Limited
Caye Financial Centre
Corner Coconut Drive & Hurricane Way
San Pedro Ambergris Caye, Belize
Tel: +501-226-3463 or +501-226-2497

Law Firms and Lawyers (source: MyBelize.net)

Arguelles & Company LLC
The Matalon, 4th Floor
Coney Drive
Belize City
Belize
Tel: +501-223-0088

Barrow & Williams
Equity House
84 Albert Street
Belize City
Belize
Tel: +501-227-5280

Courtenay Coye LLP
15 A Street, Kings Park
Belize City
Belize
Tel: +501-223-1476
Email: advice@courtenaycoye.com

Practice Areas: Constitutional & Administrative Law, Civil Litigation, Commercial & Corporate, Fraud & Asset Recovery, Real Estate Acquisition, planning and development, Tax Planning, Banking and Finance, Public Utilities & Regulatory, Offshore Company Law, Family & Relationships, Intellectual Property Law, Environmental Law, Strata Corporation Law, Estates & Succession, Tort & Personal Injuries, and Contract.

Glenn D. Godfrey & Co. LLP
35 Barrack Road
Belize City
Belize
Tel: +501-223-3530

Fred Lumor & Co.
3750 University Blvd.
Belize City
Belize
Tel: +501-223-6024

Musa & Balderamos LLP
91 North Front Street
Belize City
Belize
Tel: +501-223-2940

Estevan A. Perera
35 Barrack Road, 3rd Floor
Belize City
Belize
Tel: +501-223-3505
Email: steve@attorneybelize.com

Reyes Retreage LLP
112 Eve Street
Belize City
Belize
Tel: +501 223-2030
Email: info@lawyerbelize.com

Wrobel & Co.
115 Barrack Road, 3rd Floor
Belize City
Belize
Tel: +501-223-1013

Youngs Law Firm
28 Regent Street
Belize City
Belize
Tel: +501-227-7406

APPENDIX B

DIPLOMATIC AND GOVERNMENT CONTACTS

Canada

Belize Consulate
305 10th Ave SE
Calgary, Alberta T2G 0W2
Tel: 403-215-6072
Email: yycbelizeconsulate@mainst.biz

Bob Dhillon, Honorary Consul, Calgary, Alberta,
Tel: 403- 215-6070

United States

Belize Embassy
2535 Massachusetts Avenue NW
Washington, DC 20008
Tel: 202-332-9636
Email: reception@embassyofbelize.org
Website: www.belizeembassyusa.mfa.gov.bz

Consulate of Belize in Florida
1600 Ponce De Leon
Suite 904
Coral Gables, FL 33134
Tel: 305-755-0276
Fax: 305-755-0277
Website: www.belizeconsulflorida.com

Consular Office U.S. Embassy Belmopan
Floral Park Road
Belmopan, Cayo
Tel: +501-822-4011
Fax: +501-822-4050
Website: bz.usembassy.gov
Email: embbelize@state.gov

United Kingdom

Belize High Commission
45 Crawford Place
3rd Floor
London W1H 4LP
Tel: +44 (0)20 7723 3603
Website: belizehighcommission.co.uk
Email: info@belizehighcommission.co.uk

APPENDIX C
CRUISE SHIP ACTIVITY

Cruises are an essential part of Belize's tourism industry. While cruise passengers have a limited time to fully discover Belize, these visitors take advantage of the close proximity of tours such as snorkelling and an ancient Mayan discovery.

There are approximately 333 cruise calls to Belize annually (this and all data in this appendix are from the Belize Tourism Board). This sector continues to see steady investments in infrastructure and quality assurance to meet its growing demands.

In 2015, there was a total of 957,975 cruise passenger arrivals recorded. This was a minor dip of -1 percent when compared to 2014. In the last quarter of 2015, October recorded a drop of 29.2 percent, but there was an increase in November of 9.2 percent (81,113 passengers) and in December of 1.6 percent (143,598 passengers). During 2015, there was only one cruise call cancellation in the last quarter of the year, amounting to a total of 3,070 fewer passengers arriving to Belize. Finally, in December, Belize received the newest cruise liner — the MSC *Divina*.

Latest Data: Cruise Passenger Arrivals Register a Positive First Quarter

An overall increase of 8.7 percent in cruise passenger arrivals was recorded for the first three months of 2017. With an increase of 24.2 percent and 22.7 percent in January and February 2017 respectively, along with a short decline of 13.1 percent in March 2017, the total number of cruise ship passengers registered in the first quarter of 2017 surpassed that of 2016, giving a positive outlook for Belize's cruise tourism for the remainder of this year.

	2015	% Change vs. 2014	2016	% Change vs. 2015	2017 (partial)	% Change vs. 2016
January	127,376	16.6	102,337	-19.7	127,061	24.2
February	95,067	-2.7	98,623	3.7	120,996	22.7
March	133,482	15.8	135,283	1.3	117,578	-13.1
April	91,325	-12.3	90,657	-0.7	97,422	7.5
May	43,847	-6.4	61,977	41.3	61,152	-1.3
June	50,790	-5.6	65,399	28.8	47,007	-28.1
July	54,471	-19.9	51,968	-4.6	44,392	-14.6
August	50,656	-2.7	39,189	-22.6	52,534	34.1
September	45,265	-5.0	54,569	20.6		
October	40,985	-29.2	56,697	38.3		
November	81,113	9.2	106,144	30.9		
December	143,598	1.6	142,551	-0.7		
	957,975	-1.0	1,005,394	4.9	668,142	3.5

APPENDIX D

BELIZE FACT SHEET

Capital	Belmopan
Currency	Belize Dollar (BZ$), fixed exchange rate of BZ$2 to US$1
Ethnic Groups	Creole, Garifuna, Mestizo, Spanish, Maya, English, Mennonite, Lebanese, Chinese, and Eastern Indian
Population	387,879
Size	8,867 square miles, including 266 square miles of islands
Independence Achieved	September 21, 1981
Government	Parliamentary democracy, part of the Commonwealth of Nations (formerly the British Commonwealth)
Language	English is the official language. Spanish, Creole, Garifuna, and Mayan are also spoken
Phone Code	International access code from U.S. and Canada is 011, country code 501
Electricity	110 volts AC (same as the U.S.)
Time	GMT-6, which is the same as U.S. Central Standard Time. Daylight savings time is not observed.
Climate	Subtropical with a prevailing wind from the Caribbean Sea. Average temperature in the winter is 75° Fahrenheit, in the summer 81° Fahrenheit.

Rainfall	Annual rainfall ranges from 50 inches in the north to 170 inches in the south.
Location	Belize lies on the east coast of Central America in the heart of the Caribbean Basin. It borders Mexico to the north, Guatemala to the west and the south, and is flanked by the Caribbean Sea to the east. It is a two-hour direct flight from either Miami or Houston in the United States.
Visas	United States citizens and nationals of the European Union member nations do not require visas for short stays in the country. Visas are required for the nationals of China, Cuba, India, Libya, Pakistan, and South Africa. To obtain a visitor's permit, an application must be submitted to the Belize Immigration and Nationality Department in Belmopan, Cayo District, Belize (Tel: +501-822-2423, Fax: +501-822-2662). Visa requirements are subject to change. Please contact the Belize Embassy in the United States for up-to-date information, at 2535 Massachusetts Avenue Northwest, Washington, DC, 20008 (Tel: 202-332-9636, Fax: 202-332-6888); or Nationality Department in Belmopan, Cayo District, Belize (Tel: +501-822-2423, Fax: +501-822-2662).
Entry Requirements	A valid passport and, when necessary, a visa are required for entry into Belize. Visitors are permitted to stay in Belize for up to thirty days. For BZ$25, extensions may be granted upon application to the Immigration Office (Tel: +501-222-4620 and Fax: +501-222-4056).
Health Services	There are three hospitals in Belize City; one public and two private. Several private doctors are also available. The district towns and larger villages also have hospitals or clinics.

Water	Potable water is available in most areas of Belize, but it is advisable to ask, and, if in doubt, to drink boiled or bottled water.
Diseases	There are no serious epidemic diseases in Belize. No vaccinations are required for entry, but antimalarial tablets are recommended for extended stays in the jungle.
Taxes, Tips, and Fees	Hotel Room Tax, 9 percent. Sales tax (on goods & services), 10 percent. International Passenger Airport Departure Fee, US$39.25 (payable only in U.S. currency); International Airport to Domestic Airport Fee, US$0.75 or CAD$0.80. Boat departure to International Destination Fee, US$3.75 or CAD$3.98.
Public Holidays	New Year's Day; Baron Bliss Day, March 9; Good Friday; Holy Saturday; Easter Monday; Labour Day, May 1; Commonwealth Day, May 24; St. George's Caye Day, September 10; Independence Day, September 21; Columbus Day, October 12; Garifuna Settlement Day, November 19; Christmas Day, Boxing Day

PHOTO CREDITS

Alamy: 24

Belize Tourism Board: 9, 152, 156

Beth Clifford: 58 (top and bottom)

BNE: 190, 192

Kelsey Blackwell: 146 (top)

Dimitri Ioudine: 107, 108

Marius Jovaša, Heavenly Belize: 42 (top), 128 (top), 159, 182, 187

Fred Langan: 63 (top and bottom), 66, 81, 116 (top and bottom), 122, 123, 128 (bottom), 133, 139, 149, 160, 162, 184

Maya Island Air: 45, 146 (bottom), 198

Statistical Institute of Belize: 185

Tony Rath of Tony Rath Photography: 27, 29, 40, 42 (bottom), 147 (top and bottom), 153, 154

INDEX

The letter *t* following a page number denotes a table.

Abdul-Jabbar, Kareem, 137
Actun Tunichil Muknal (ATM), 31
affordability, 7–8, 16, 35, 74, 92, *128*, 142–43, 169
agriculture, 38, *182*, 183–84, *185*, 186–87
airlines, 7, 19, 53–56, 66, 74, 122, *146*, 195–99
airports, 7, 44, *45*, 70, 73–74, 128, 145, 195–99, 202
Althuna Temple, *29*
Amber Sunset Jungle Resort, 19
Ambergris Caye, 7, 15, 19, 43–45, 52–53, 62, 73–75, 124, 127, 136–37, 157–58, 197, 202–03
archaeology, 26, *27*, *29*, 30, 41
artists, 66–67
Atlantic International Bank, 101, 103–04, 113, 132
Azul, 18
baby boomers, 89, 167
backpackers, 35, 74, 144
bananas, 38–39, 181t, 183–84, *185*, 186
Bank of Nova Scotia, *107*
banking, 103–04, 106, *107*, *108*, 109–10, 112–13, 117–18, 165
  See also Atlantic International Bank; Bank of Nova Scotia; Choice Bank; Inter-American Development Bank; Scotiabank
Barbados, 16t, 43, 126
Barrow, Dean, 99
Bay of Honduras, 23–24
Belize, 82, *128*, *149*
  area, 16, 38, 157
  atmosphere, 51
  constitution, 98
  currency, *15*, 59, 103, 106, 108–10, 165
  GDP, per capita, 16t

geography, 8, 17, 20–21, 43
government, 100, 102
key features, 90–91
legal system, 8, 10, 56, 90–91, 100, 117, 201–02
literacy rate, 32
maps, *9*
population, 16t, 17, 19–20, 25, 33t, 73, 83, 121, 187
Belize: A Concise History (Thompson), 22, 32–33
Belize Barrier Reef, 40, 43, 47, 150–52, 164
Belize City, 7, 21, 38, *116*, 169, 198
Belize Harbour, *24*
Belize Natural Energy, 188–89, *190*, 191–92
Belize River, 38t
Belize Tourism Board, 170–71, 175
Belizean Arts gallery, 65, *66*, 67–69
Belmopan, 38, 189
Beltraide, 92, 180
Berman, Joshua, 99
birdwatching, 35, 38, 41, *42*, 83, *154*, 155
Blackadore Caye, 134–35
Blackbeard, 22
Blackbird Caye, *123*, 142, 158, 163–64
Blue Hole Natural Monument, 43–44
BNE Trust, 190
boutique developers, 59, 202
boutique resorts, 18, 144
See also resorts
Brahma Blue, 18–19, 125–26, 135, 195
Britain
Belize, role in, 23–26, 76
Spain, treaty with, 23
British common law, 8, 10, 14
British Honduras. *See* Belize
Brown Sugar Market Place, 101
Burnaby, Rear Admiral, 23
business, 57, 68, 94, 114, 179, 181–82
See also export processing zones
business environment, 91–92, 100–101, 204

Caana, 42
Cahal Pech, *29*
Calgary
Forest Lawn District, 81–82
call centres, 200
Campbell, Brad, 125
Canada, 13–14, 74, 76, 81–82, 84, 90, 94, 100, 120, 166, 168, 172
Cancún, 18, 127, 144
Caracol, 26, *29*, 42
Caribbean region, 13, 47, 71, 143
CasasdelaCayevillas.com, 125
casinos, 199–200
cave tubing, 130, 155
Caye Caulker, 35, 38, 74–75, 124, 127, 129, 158, *159–60*, 161–62, 193, 197–98, 202
Cayes. *See* islands
Cayo district, 130, 166, *182*

Cayo Espanto, 35
Central America, 13–14, 21, 59, 71, 123–24
Choice Bank, 107, 109
Choudhary, Bhoj Raj, 190–91
Clifford, Beth, 57–62
Coastal Living, 61
Cockscomb Basin Wildlife Sanctuary, 41
Colombia, 7
commercial free zone, 180–81
condominiums, 43, 44, 123, 133
construction, 53, 61–62, 123–25, 137–40
Corozal, 129
Corozal Free Zone, 180–81
correspondent banking, 113
cost of living, 7–8, 44, 97
Costa del Sol, 18–20, 37, 46, *122*, 124–26, *133*, 135, 138, *139*, 143, 194, 196, 202
Costa Rica, 13–14, 16t, 17, 20, 39, 119, 167
Coye, Christopher, 112–13
Cozumel, 127
credit cards, 104, 109, 118, 165
Creole, 33t
crime, 166
cruises, 127, *156*
culture, 67
currency, *15*, 103, 106, 108–10, 121, 165

Dangriga, 129
demand, demographics of, 72–75, 84–85
democracies
  wealth of, 93
Deol, Jaspal, 143, 194–95
deposit rates, 111
  See also interest rates
development, 18, 20, 25, 39, 84, 135–36
  Ambergris Caye, 19, 52–53, 57, *58*, 136–37, 202
  Blackbird Caye, 164
  boutique style, 18, 59
  encouraging, 91
  Mahogany Bay, 60–62
  See also projects and development
Dhillon, Bob, 79–80, *81*, 96, 120–22, *139*
DiCaprio, Leonardo, 134
diversity, 99
diving, 34, 39, 43–44, 83, *147*, *152*, 164, 201
dual citizenship, 69
duty-free shopping, 75–76, 117–18

eco-tourism, *147*, 148
economic incentives, 179–81
Economist, 89, 142–43
Egypt, 93–94
El Castillo, 26
El Pilar, *29*
El Salvador, 38, 59
elections, 98
electricity, 42, 44, 53, 55–56, 82, 97, 138, 142–43, 166, 168, 193–95
emerging markets, 59, 195
English, 17, 51, 72, 76
entrepreneurship, 77, 90–91, 157, 179

environmentalism, 91, 135, 137–38, 140–42, 153
ethnicity
Belize, 99
Euros (currency), 103–04, 106, 110, 121
exclusive economic zones, 197
export processing zones, 179–80
exports, 181t, 182–83, *185*, 186–87

farming, 129–30
Fay, Ab, 51–54
fees
activities, 155
banking, 107
business, 102–03, 181
incorporating, 94, 114–15
passport, 172
property, 43–45, 124
retirement, 176–77
stamp tax, 132
fishing, *147*, 201
Florida, 59–60, 128
free enterprise, 93
free trade, 181
free-title ownership, 56, 90
See also land title

Gallery of San Pedro, 67
gambling, 199–200
Garifuna, 32, 33t, 129
gated communities, 127–28
Glover's Atoll, *116*, 150
golf, 129
government. *See under* Belize
Grand Caribe, 73
Grand Cayman, 73
Great Blue Hole, 39, *40*, 43–44, 163
Grimshaw, Tom, 30
Guatemala, 8, 17, 25, 75, 94–95
Guerrero, Danny, 19, 73, 136–37, 166

Hackston, Lindsey, 65, *66*, 67–69
Hakimi, Karim, 19
Harvest Caye, 156
Heredia, Manuel, 17, 46, 156–57, 159–60, 195–97
Hermit Caye, 126
Hernán Cortés, 21
Hilton Hotels
Curio Collection, 60
history, 21, 22t, 23–25, 97, 163
Mayan, 16, 26–31
Hol Chan Marine Reserve, 41
Honduras, 59, 94–95
honeymoon tourism, 156–58
Hopkins, 127, 129
hot sauce, 75
Hotchandani, Bob, 101
hotels, 18–19, 60–62, 69–70, 121, 145
See also Victoria House Hotel
housing, designs of, 20, 123–24, 126, 135, 138–41
hurricanes, 20, 37, 140–41, 159, 163

imports, 181t
inheritances, 89

Inter-American Development Bank, 183
interest rates, 103–04, 111, 131
See also deposit rates
international banks, 107–11, 113–14, 122, 131, 204
See also banking
International Business Companies (IBC) program, 101–03, 114–15, 118, 169, 204
International Living, 72, 92, 97, 167
internet connectivity, 35, 77, 102, 118, 142
investment, 85, 89, 201
investors, types of, 20
Ioudine, Dmitri, 76–77
islands, 8, 37, *149*, 158–59

jaguars, *153*, 154
Jamaica, 43
jet-setters, 34–35
JYOTO, 64–65

Kanantik Reef and Jungle Resort, 153
Kazi, Zubair, 186–87
Key, Mervin, 52
Kirchberger, Gabriel, 18–19, 125–26, 135, 139, 194–95

La Sirene, 137, 203
labour costs, 124–25
Lamanal, *29*
land prices, 52, 59, 83, 124, 126, 132, 134
land title, 13–14, 76–77, 93–94, 131, 133–34
languages
English, 17, 51, 76–77
Spanish, 15, 17
Lansing, Jerry, 67
legal systems
Belize, 8, 10, 56, 90–92, 100, 117, 201–02
Costa Rica, 14
life span, 89–90
Lighthouse Reef, 150, *152*
loans, 111, 131
logwood, 22–23
lumber, 23, 61, 139–40, 188

Macal River, 38*t*
mahogany, 23, 139–40, 188
Mahogany Bay, 57, *58*, 60–62, 203
Mainstreet Equity Corporation, 81–82, 84
mangroves, *147*, 148–49
maps, *9*, *146*
marinas, 127
Mata Resort, *116*
Maya Island Air, 37, *45*, *146*, 184, 198–99
Mayan ruins, 16, 26, *27*, *29*, 31, 42, 130, 201
Maya, 21, 26–31, 33t, 41, 45
measurement units, 166
medical services, 35, 90, 165, 169
Meighan, Danny, 69
Meighan, Jeremy, 69–70, 136
Mennonites, 33t, 139, *182*, 183
Mestizos, 33t
Mexico, 8, 13–14, 16–17, 45, 75, 191

micro-businesses, 62–65
Monkey River, 38t
Morrice, Susan, 188–90, *192*, 193
mortgages, 105–06, 111
Mountain Pine Ridge, 42
Mystery of Capital, The: Why Capitalism Triumphs in the West and Fails Everywhere Else (Soto), 93–94

national parks, 39–41
New York Times, 134
Nicaragua, 59
North China Shipping Company, 80, 96
Nsiah-Perovic, Joyce, 62, *63*

oil, 188–91
Orange Walk, district of, 129

Paradise Shrimp Farm, 187
parks, 39–42
Pasta Per Caso, 161, *162*
Pau, Anna, 161–63
Pau, Armando, 161–63
Pelayo, Giovanni, 19
Pelayo, Ricardo, 19, 111–13
Placencia, 7, 74, 127–28, 196
Platinum Coast, 37, 134–36, 203
population groups, 33t, 66–67, 99
private aircraft, 168, 175, 197, 201
private property, 15–16, 170
projects and development, 18, 19, 52–53, 57, *58*, 84, 136–37, 202
See also development
property ownership, 15–16, 76–77, 93–94, 131–33
property taxes, 44, 103–04

Qualified Retired Persons Program, 103, 117–18, 167–71, 174–78, 181

Rainbow Grill and Bar, 161
rainforest, 42
Rasta Pasta Rainforest Café, 161
RE/MAX, 71–72
real estate, 71–72, 89, 119–20, *128*
buying, 126–27, 130–33
in Canada, 80, 83–84
money-saving, 82, 142
purchasing in Belize, 105
Reardon-Smith, Simon, 75–76, 161
Redneck Riviera, 59–60
reefs, 69, *147*, 149–50
See also Belize Barrier Reef; Blue Hole Natural Monument
Registered Land Act System, 131, 133
rentals, 43, 61, 82–84, 125–26
residency laws, 92, 98, 103
resorts, 18–19, 29, 35, 59–60, 62, 69–70, 72–73, *116*, 123, 129, 134, 143–44, 153, 199–200
restaurants, 46–47, 59, 62, 64–65, 75, 137, 161, *162*

Retired Persons (Incentives) (Amendment) Act, 2001, 174–77
retirement, 68, 89–90, 103, 117–21, 127, 167–71, 173–74, 201
program, 98, 103, 117–18
See also Qualified Retired Persons Program
Rice, Browne, 51–52, 54
Richard Ivey School of Business, 77, 80–81
Riley, Robert, 148–51
rivers, 38t, *42*
Rojo Lounge, 157

safety, 46
San Ignacio, 17, 38, 130
San Pedro, 15, 17–18, 38, 43–47, 56, 60, *107*, 124–25, 127, 136, 140, 151
Sapodilla Cayes, 158
scenery, 37, 129, 135, 153–54, 160, 201
Scotiabank, *107*
Secret Beach, 137
septic systems, 124, 141
Sharp, Marie, 75
shrimp, *187*
Sibun River, 38t, 40–41
Sikhs, 79, 96
Sittee River, 38t
snowbirds, 34
solar power, 97, 137–38, 142–43, 194–95
Soto, Hernado de, 93–94
The Mystery of Capital: Why Capitalism Triumphs in the West and Fails Everywhere Else, 93–94
Spanglish, 17
Spanish civil code, 14
Spanish Lookout, *182*, *190*
Spanish speakers, 15, 17
Spiegel, Jeff, 18
Squatters' rights, 16, 170
St. George's Caye, Battle of, 23–34
St. Herman's Blue Hole National Park, 40–41
St. Herman's Cave, 41
stamp tax, 132
Stann Creek District, 126, 129
survey systems, 10, 122, 132–33
sushi, 64
sustainability, 138–40, 149–51
See also environmentalism

taxes, 103–04, 112, 114, 131
property, 44, 103–04
retirees, 10, 90–91, 168–69, 174
stamp tax, 132
Teach, William. *See* Blackbeard
teak, 139–40, 188
Thompson, P.A.B., 32–33
Belize: A Concise History, 22
Thuraiaiyah, Shiromi, 132
tolerance, in Belize, 97
Torrens system, 131, 133
tourism, 18–20, 46, 56, 72, 121–22, 144, 145t, *147*, 150, 152–53, 156–58, 182, 199, 203–04
travel times, *146*, 166, 195, *198*

travellers, common types, 34–35
Tropic Air, 37, 45, 198
trusts, 115, 117
Trusts Act (1992), 115
Tsujimoto, Toshiya, 64–65
Turley, John, 62, 71–74
Turneffe Atoll, 22–23, 150, 163–64
Turneffe Island Resort, 19

Undersea World of Jacques Cousteau, The, 43
United Nations World Heritage Committee (UNESCO), 43
United States
  currency, *15*, 106, 108
  visa requirements from, 172–73
Unitedville, 19
Usher, Mike, 189
Utrera, Carlos, 77

Victoria House Hotel, 51–57, 157, 203
visa requirements 172–73
visitors, respect for, 15
voting rights, in Belize, 90, 98, 100, 169

Wall Street Journal, 121
Wallace, Peter, 21–22
waste water, 141
Water Jets International, 45
wealth
  Belize, 94–95
  and democracies, 93–95
weather, 20, 36t, 37, 39
  See also hurricanes
weekend getaway travellers, 34
WestJet, 19
wildlife, 35, 40, 46, 135, *153*, *154*, 154, 155
Wood, Sally, 155
World Bank rankings, 101t
World Heritage Sites, 40, 43, 152
Wyndham Hotel, 69–70, 136

Yucatán Peninsula, 20

Zabaneh, Eugene, 183–86, *184*, 198–99